STARTING AND RUNNING A
Coaching Business

'As someone who has hired coaches, been coached, now coaches others, and has run a viable business for the last two years, I can only say that I wish Aryanne had written her book sooner. While there are many business start-up texts, for the coach thinking of setting up on their own, this packs genuine, practical advice into every page and is likely to become a definitive reference. It will confront you with the truth about setting up on your own – and sometimes not pull any punches with that. It's there to keep you focused, and is just as useful to read when you're 12 months into your business as when you're starting out.'
DAMIAN GRIFFITHS | Director VProfessional
Former IT Director Addleshaw Goddard and Eversheds

'This is a book that presents an often complex topic in a logical, easy to read and readily digestible way that is immediately useful to anyone busy setting up their business. In particular the clear, concise chapters and sub-sections allow the reader to easily identify and focus on a particular area of interest, without having necessarily to read the entire book in one go. It can therefore be used informally as a "user manual" or as a formal, technical book. If you are setting up – or are thinking about setting up – a coaching business, or for that matter any other small business, I recommend it – highly.'
ADRIAN OLSEN | Managing Director and Head of Global Project Finance
Bank of Ireland Corporate Banking

'I would readily recommend this book to anyone thinking of setting up their own business, whether or not it is in the field of coaching. It covers the whole spectrum of what it takes to organise and run your own enterprise. The book is both a reference and a learning tool that takes you through the process of understanding everything about setting up your practice and also your own motivations for doing so. By posing a series of key questions in each chapter, you are continuously encouraged to reflect on how you approach and deal with each aspect of your business. Based on many years of solid experience in the coaching industry, the writer offers useful insights, encouragement and support. The book is packed with both invaluable advice and a good deal of common sense.'
RANDINI WANDURAGALA | Consultant Shared Profits
Former Head of Policy World Vision UK
Former Advocacy Manager Asia Tsunami Response Team World Vision International

'This book will prove useful to both experienced and newly qualified coaches who are thinking about setting up their own business. It is pragmatic with its advice, and also thought provoking. A good practical read.'
LINDA GRANT | Leadership Development Manager
Skipton Building Society

'This is a comprehensive and insightful guide, full of practical ideas and suggestions. It will be a useful toolkit for the newly qualified or the experienced coach.'
STEVE PRESTON | HR Director, Learning and Development
An investment bank

Please send for a free copy of the latest catalogue:

How To Books
Spring Hill House, Spring Hill Road,
Begbroke, Oxford OX5 1RX, United Kingdom
info@howtobooks.co.uk
www.howtobooks.co.uk

STARTING AND RUNNING A

Coaching Business

The Complete Guide to Setting Up and Managing a Coaching Practice

Aryanne Oade

howtobooks / **smallbusinessstart-ups**

Published by How To Books Ltd,
Spring Hill House, Spring Hill Road,
Begbroke, Oxford OX5 1RX, United Kingdom
Tel: (01865) 375794 Fax: (01865) 379162
info@howtobooks.co.uk
www.howtobooks.co.uk

How To Books greatly reduce the carbon footprint of their books by sourcing their typesetting and printing in the UK.

First edition 2009

British Library Cataloguing in Publication Data.
A catalogue record for this book is available from the British Library.

ISBN 978 1 84528 332 2

Produced for How To Books by Deer Park Productions, Tavistock
Printed and bound by Cromwell Press Ltd, Trowbridge, Wiltshire

NOTE: The material contained in this book is set out in good faith for general guidance and no liability can be accepted for loss or expense incurred as a result of relying in particular circumstances on statements made in the book. Laws and regulations are complex and liable to change, and readers should check the current position with the relevant authorities before making personal arrangements.

CONTENTS

ACKNOWLEDGEMENTS

I would like to acknowledge a number of people who have played a part in my work and in the writing of this book.

My gratitude and thanks go first and foremost to all the clients with whom I have worked over the years, and from whom I have learned so much as they talked with me about their working lives and experiences.

Next, I'd like to express my appreciation to my actor colleague Tim Scragg for creating credible corporate and professional services characters in coaching meetings, and for his incisive and thoughtful critique of the book at its draft stage.

My gratitude and thanks also go to my accountant of many years Nadine Lamont-Brown for her humour and prompt, helpful responses to my numerous enquiries and queries, and for her review of Chapter 10.

My thanks go to my supervisor Christine Marklow for the clinical psychology perspective she provides me with during our supervision meetings, and for her critique of Chapter 6.

Agnes Moodie got me started on the book in the first place and for that I will always be grateful. My thanks also go to Giles Lewis and Nikki Read at How To Books for suggesting that I write a book on setting up and managing a coaching practice, and, when I sent them my preliminary outline, for sending me a publishing contract rather than a request for more information.

In addition, I send my gratitude to the members of my EFT Group for their support while I wrote the book. I'm thankful to Julie Perry and Sally Thomas for helping me find my words again when they had stopped flowing, to Sarah Granby for her time in proof-reading, and to Julie Perry again for her work in reviewing Chapter 9.

Finally, thanks to all the people who spoke with me about the challenges of running their emerging coaching practices, including Dave Bareham and Jane Waites who helpfully detailed for me, as I started to write, the questions and issues going round their heads as they prepared to set up their coaching businesses.

NOTE FROM THE AUTHOR

This book focuses your attention on ten key aspects of starting and running your coaching practice. In writing the book, I am not seeking to advise you, the reader, on how to set up your business, but rather to offer you my experiences and know-how as someone who started, and has managed, a coaching practice for many years. In addition to reading the book, you might want to seek the services and professional advice of a lawyer, accountant and/or independent financial advisor, each of whom will be able to offer you tailored, detailed and impartial counsel on your business' requirements.

ABOUT THE AUTHOR

Aryanne Oade has worked as a Chartered Psychologist since 1991. She has appeared on C4 speaking about customer complaints handling, has given an address on 'Creativity in Business' at the British Association for the Advancement of Science and has appeared on Radio 4 speaking on the same topic. Aryanne has spoken twice at the Institute of Directors Yorkshire Breakfast Meetings on 'Politics, Power and Profit', and once at the British Psychological Society's Annual Conference on 'Stress Levels Among South Yorkshire Probation Officers'. She holds memberships in the British Psychological Society's Occupational Psychology Division and Special Group in Coaching Psychology. She is a Member of the Association for Coaching as well as the European Mentoring and Coaching Council.

OVERVIEW

Who this book is for

I have written this book for you if you have thought long and hard about starting up a coaching business and have decided to go ahead, or if you are considering starting and running a coaching business and want to know more about what will be involved. You may be on the way towards a professional coaching qualification, or already have achieved either accreditation or part-accreditation as a coach. You may be moving into coaching from a learning and development, internal coaching or human resources background, or after working as a line manager. Or you may be a psychologist working in business, as I am. You could be moving into coaching from a different and, possibly, unrelated field. You may have gained experience of working as a coach during your training, already worked as an internal coach, read several books on coaching, talked to effective and successful coaches, and may have experienced helpful coaching yourself at some stage in your career or life.

You may now believe that your life and workplace experiences have prepared you to be an effective and professional coach, one who will find the work both rewarding and challenging, one who has something valuable to offer to clients. You likely see coaching as a way of assisting other people to grow and develop so that they achieve their goals. Above all, you are feeling excited by the prospect of running your own business, being your own boss, and working in a role that will bring you into contact with stimulating people on a regular basis – your clients who represent the great richness, variety and depth there is in everyday people; and other coaches who work in similar and different niches to yourself.

So, you are exploring what will be involved in setting up and running your own coaching business. You have many questions and issues competing for your attention and head space. Some of these questions may only abate when you take action; others could need thinking through before you do anything. Your questions might include:

☐ If I am to work as a coach, how will I find my clients?

☐ What will I say to prospective clients when I talk about what I do?

☐ What can I offer clients anyway, even with a coaching qualification?

☐ How will my coaching offer differ from the many similar offers already out there?

1

☐ What will clients expect from me?

☐ Who will I market to and how will I do it?

☐ How will I structure my coaching offer?

☐ How will I measure the outcomes of my coaching programmes?

☐ Can I really make a living as a coach?

☐ What will I charge for my services?

☐ How much am I worth anyway?

☐ What competition do I have?

☐ What standards of ethical and professional practice do I need to adhere to?

☐ What insurance do I need?

☐ Do I need a business plan?

☐ How do I handle my tax?

☐ What about VAT?

☐ What does my coaching qualification mean to potential clients?

☐ What does it mean to me?

☐ How am I going to make this happen, happen well and make a living from it?

My background and coaching experience

I am a Chartered Occupational Psychologist. I began working as a business psychologist in the late 1980s. Over a five-year period I worked for three consultancy firms based in different parts of the UK and my work mainly involved designing and delivering professional skills workshops. In early 1994 I decided to leave paid employment and set up as an independent coach, workshop facilitator and consultant. I had two main reasons for doing this. Firstly, I wanted to offer clients a confidential, one-to-one coaching service that would enable them to develop their leadership and management skills, and help them make sustained behaviour changes in key areas. Secondly, I wanted my energy and commitment to go wholly towards working with clients, rather than partly towards working with clients and partly towards managing colleague relationships and the political elements of organizational life. To this end I decided to set up as an independent business psychologist.

Some of my initial projects were carried out as an associate to smaller consultancy firms. In January 2000 I set up Oade Associates to design and deliver bespoke executive coaching programmes, tailored professional skills workshops and custom-made conference scenarios. In this work I combine business psychology with the skills of professional actors to create scenarios that mirror the real-life issues that my clients deal with in their professional relationships. Since starting Oade Associates, I have run over 130 tailored coaching programmes and over 100 professional skills workshops for managers and leaders working in, mainly, professional services firms and financial services firms across the UK, Europe and North America.

In my coaching programmes and workshops, I ask clients to step back from their day-to day work and their key business relationships and reflect on the quality of the behaviour they use when things are going well for them, and compare that to what they do when they are under pressure. Then, with the help of my professional actor colleagues, I recreate the very meetings that clients find most challenging – meetings which they mishandle, or in which they lose influence or credibility – and help them to revisit these meetings using different and more productive behaviours, skills and interpersonal tactics. I coach them to understand the links between their intra-personal world (their values, character and personality) and their inter-personal world (the behaviour, skills and strategies that they use with other people). Clients then have the opportunity to practise their new approaches until they are satisfied that they can go back to work and use them straight away. As a result of working in this way clients perform better in their roles, have greater influence in their key workplace relationships and demonstrate sustained behaviour change.

I live on a farm in Yorkshire from where I run my business. This means that I can work with clients in a country location, away from their busy offices. Clients find this change of context both stimulating and helpful. It enables them to reflect on the effectiveness of their workplace behaviour and look for performance improvements away from the day-to-day distractions of their places of work.

What this book will do for you

This book comes directly from my experiences as a coach. In it, I have distilled for you what I have learnt, what I consider to be key issues for you as a new coach and as someone running a business possibly for the first time. In reading it I want to help you answer some of the questions that might be going through your mind and, hopefully, point you towards a few more that you also need to consider. My aim throughout is to give you as many tips, ideas, pointers and heads-up suggestions as I can so that your main focus, and your energy, can be directed towards the key thing that an effective coach does: working with clients to help them make progress towards their coaching goals. You will still need to run, manage, market and handle your business. But, in writing this book, I'd like to help you make these parts of your working life as straightforward as possible, so that you can focus on your passion: finding and coaching clients.

In the course of the various chapters we'll address all the questions listed above, and several more. This will also assist you in making the most of the opportunity you have to run your own business, allowing you to use your precious time as effectively as possible and to make sure that your focus stays where it should be – on working with your clients. What a book like this can't do is make up for any coaching skills shortfalls you may have, or any lack of competency on your part in running your business. But it will show you how to make sure that you keep your eye on the two key issues before you in starting and running a coaching business:

☐ How do you convince potential clients to work with you as opposed to any of the other coaches out there?

☐ How do you stay on top of the essentials in running a small business, given that the majority of your time and energy needs to be spent finding and working with clients?

Periodically, you will come upon a series of questions that you may wish to consider and answer in relation to your coaching business. Each question is followed by a space in the text so that you can jot down your answers if you want to. These questions will provide you with an opportunity to apply the key points from the previous sections of the book to your business and should also help you to get the most you can out of this material.

Who will benefit from the book

Each of the chapters that follows is on a different, but related, aspect of starting and running a coaching business. I have written the book for anyone who has concerns that they have:

☐ effective coaching skills, but lack the confidence to run a coaching business;

☐ a coaching qualification, but don't know how to get a business off the ground;

☐ passion and enthusiasm for running a coaching business, but are worried that, in doing so, they might have bitten off more than they can chew.

However, this is also a book for those people who are undaunted about setting up and running a coaching business, and who:

□ want a heads-up about the key issues they will face in the weeks and months ahead;

□ simply want to find out what someone else has learnt from the process they are currently going through.

I will touch on important issues such as marketing, selling and managing your business finances. However, this book is not intended as a comprehensive guide to these specific aspects of running a business, and you may also want to consult a few of the many excellent books available that focus wholly on these issues.

Your coaching business

My hope is that you will use this book to help you step back from the day-to-day work of setting up and running your coaching business and thereby review *the way you are going about it*. At the end of the day it's your business and you are responsible for it. It will necessarily take on your character and your values. You will make the decisions and it's you alone who will make it work for you and your clients. I designed this book to take you through a process of thinking about different aspects of your business. Therefore, it will encourage you to:

□ focus on the key issues you need to attend to;

□ stop wasting your time and effort on peripheral issues;

□ invest your energy and commitment where this will provide the best return for you and your clients.

My wish is that your coaching business takes off, that you enjoy the challenge of finding and working with clients, and that you can overcome the inevitable setbacks and let downs you will experience. But, above all, I hope that your clients report that working with you helps them to clarify what they need to do differently and better, and equips them with the know-how, skills, tools and mindsets they need to help them achieve their coaching goals.

1
RUNNING YOUR OWN COACHING BUSINESS

So you want to run a coaching business or, at the very least, are actively exploring the possibility of doing so. If you do take the plunge and start a small business offering coaching services, what can you expect from your first steps in charge of your own practice?

The aim of this chapter is to take you through some of the key issues you will face as you go it alone as a coach, running a business possibly for the first time. Specifically, it focuses on the three key and interrelated issues of:

☐ working as a coach;

☐ being your own boss;

☐ assuming complete responsibility for both of these things.

Let's start by getting you to step back from your day-to-day activity and consider what has led you to want to set up and run a coaching business. I'd like you to consider the most basic question of all: 'Why do you want to coach?'

Why do you want to coach?

As you may be well on the way to setting up a coaching practice, or may have been running one for some time now, it may seem a bit odd, not to mention late, for me to ask you to revisit why you want to coach. However, I would like you to do just that. I'd like you to ask yourself what attracted you to coaching in the first place, and what continues to attract you towards coaching now. I'd like you to think about these two things before you read on. You can use the space below to jot down your ideas or you may want to use a separate notebook.

‘

’

WHY MANY PEOPLE BECOME INDEPENDENT COACHES

Take a look at the list below which captures some of the reasons that so many people are drawn to work as an independent coach.

Coaching represents a way of:

- ☐ working with, and investing in, other people's lives;

- ☐ contributing to a process of positive change for other people;

- ☐ giving back to the world of work in terms of the time, effort, energy and commitment required to help other people develop;

- ☐ being involved in an ongoing process of learning and development for yourself and your clients;

- ☐ using your own experience and skills positively to assist other people;

- ☐ having greater autonomy, flexibility, choice and independence over whom you work with and in what way;

- ☐ getting out of corporate life and organizational politics;

- ☐ retaking control of your own working life after years of only having partial control as an employee;

- ☐ making more money than your previous role enabled you to;

- ☐ running your own business, being your own boss.

All of these reasons, and others, motivate people to train, qualify and work as an independent coach. You may relate to many of them, some of them, or none of them at all. My note of caution is this: I believe that at the heart of an effective coach is someone who wants to help their clients with the issues that they are equipped to help them with. Of course a coach needs to earn a living, wants to make money from coaching, and wants to enjoy their work. But an effective coach has to be committed primarily to creating a relationship in which they assist their client with the issues that the client is paying the coach to assist them with. To be effective, a coach needs to build a coaching relationship with each of his or her clients which will result in the client:

☐ defining their key coaching goals;

☐ resolving their key coaching issues;

☐ finding answers to their key coaching questions;

☐ clarifying what they need to do differently and better;

☐ being able to take the actions and steps which will result in them achieving those goals.

An effective coach must build a productive working relationship with every one of his or her clients, and to do so has to invest in each client relationship from its inception to the closure of the coaching relationship. For some clients, this process will take a few hours and only one or two coaching meetings. For other clients it will require a much longer period of time. The challenge for a coach is to remain genuinely interested, supportive and appropriately challenging of a client throughout the time they work together. In other words, to give of their best, a coach needs to be genuinely interested in the life, working world, challenges, pressures, goals, hopes and fears of each of their clients.

For a coach who is motivated, at least partly, by wanting to contribute positively to other people's working lives, this will be an easy and natural thing to do. For a coach who sees their clients as primarily a route to financial reward or professional status this will not be easy, and for some it may not be possible at all. In these cases, clients will quickly realise that their coach's effort isn't fully engaged with the business of assisting them. Few clients will want to be on the receiving end of such coaching for very long.

Why do you want to be your own boss?

A second key question for the new coach working as a sole practitioner is 'Why do you want to be your own boss?' Before they start to run their own coaching business, many new coaches are highly motivated by the very real delights of being their own boss. They see the switch from paid employment to self-employment as one that involves freedom, autonomy, independence and more workplace flexibility than most employed people experience. In opting for these exciting benefits, new coaches can overlook the very real flip side of the coin: that they are also alone, assuming total responsibility for generating their own income, assuming total responsibility for identifying and solving their own problems, and assuming total responsibility for making all the decisions that need to be made in their businesses.

For some coaches who are used to being part of lengthy workplace decision-making and problem-solving processes – involving several people and hours of debate – the freedom to decide and choose can be exciting, even exhilarating. For others, though, it can come as quite a shock and can create a degree of nervousness and anxiety that as a new coach they were not expecting.

For most coaches, however, the reality of working for themselves is a breath of fresh air. It means that as a new coach they can:

☐ get things done without having to go through other people;

☐ make decisions speedily and effectively without having to consult;

☐ determine for themselves what they need to do and simply do it, without having to justify their preferred course of action to anyone else;

☐ employ their effort and their energies towards making things happen, rather than try to influence other people to agree that they ought to happen;

☐ enjoy the lack of restraints, constraints and restrictions that come with operating independently.

The risks that go with this degree of autonomy don't tend to figure too highly in new coaches' thinking initially and they will enjoy their freedom as a result. Rather than being daunted, or even rendered incapable by it, many new coaches thrive in the new-found freedom that being their own boss brings. Coaches who take to being their own boss straightaway can really enjoy the room to manoeuvre, the opportunities they have to get things done, the space they have to think and act as they want, and the possibility of working in a way that is comfortable for them as individuals. The reality can really be as good as they hoped it would be. Hopefully, this is you. But if it isn't, and you are daunted or uncertain by the autonomy you have as your own boss, my wish is that the rest of this book will help you think through how to handle yourself, your business and your clients so that you can realize the goals you have set for yourself – the same goals which encouraged you to qualify as a coach in the first place.

The upsides of working as your own boss

So, what does working as your own boss mean to you? Are you revelling in the choices you have, or somewhat daunted by all the possibilities for getting it wrong? I'd like you to start by thinking of all the positive aspects to working as your own boss before you read on. You can use the space below to jot down your ideas, or you may prefer to use a separate notebook.

‘

’

We will be visiting all the possible downsides of working as your own boss in the following chapters, but, for now, let's stick to the good news. Working as your own boss has many upsides to it in addition to the freedom and choice discussed above. These include:

- ☐ seeing yourself moving steadily towards the business goals and objectives you've set for yourself, and enjoying your successes along the way;

- ☐ contributing to your own personal development through taking on the challenge of running your own business;

- ☐ learning new business skills such as accounting, selling, marketing and advertising;

- ☐ deciding on the ongoing professional skills development you'd like to have and pursuing those options;

- ☐ being able to spend your own budgets as you see fit;

- ☐ taking the risks and exploiting the opportunities you want;

- ☐ being able to choose which suppliers, if any, to work with and in what way;

- ☐ deciding what to call your coaching business and what its core coaching services will be;

- ☐ deciding which clients to market to and how to go about that marketing;

- ☐ establishing a more favourable work–life balance;

- ☐ having the opportunity to take holidays when you need or want them.

All of these positive reasons, as well as others, motivate new coaches to work on their own. You may relate to many of them, some of them or none of them at all. My note of caution is this: for all the very clear benefits of working for yourself, you are likely to be the only person you can turn to, the only person you can consult and the only person you can hold accountable should things not go well for you over a particular issue. While I think it vital that every coach establishes and maintains effective peer relationships with other coaches, some of whom will prove able sounding boards for your more challenging decisions and problems, at the end of the day it is you who are solely responsible for managing, marketing and running your business.

Enjoying the rewards

Hopefully, it will go well for you and you will enjoy the rewards – professional and personal – of becoming an able coach and running an effective coaching practice. However, should things start to become difficult for you, you will need to draw on all your tenacity, resourcefulness and determination to turn things around. My hope is that the remaining chapters of this book will provide you with pointers which will help you prevent some things going wrong for you, help you focus on the key issues before you and allow you to make the most of what you have: a passion for coaching, for learning and for contributing to a process which results in your clients developing and growing, and you having a rewarding and satisfying business. Let's start by looking at how you define your coaching offer.

2

DEFINING YOUR COACHING OFFER

No matter how you look at it, you are the product you are selling. As a coach, it is you that the client has to want to work with. Whether every coaching meeting you design and deliver is bespoke, or whether your coaching is structured around a set process, a client has to want to work with *you* as opposed to any of the many other coaches out there. If a potential client doesn't feel comfortable with you – or, depending on the size of the organization they work for, if their manager, learning and development or human resource partner don't think that you will deliver effectively – they will choose to work with someone else. It's as simple as that.

The key question for you therefore is: in what ways are you going to invest time in convincing potential clients that working with you is the best bet for them? It isn't enough for you to believe that your coaching material and skills are top notch, although it's a good place to start. Your potential clients have to believe it, so that they will decide to work with you and not another coach. The aim of this chapter is to point you in the right direction so you can:

☐ decide how to describe your coaching offer to your potential clients;

☐ make decisions about how you want to invest quality time with each potential client you speak to so you can get as much business as you'd like.

The chapter will help you to determine how you want to speak with, handle and work with potential clients so that they begin to see you as someone worth working with. It will also help you decide on what way to describe your coaching services in order that the outcomes from working with you are clear to your potential clients and encourage them to hire you as their coach.

You are your own product

You need to see yourself as 'the product' you are offering. This is essential if you are to take advantage of all the opportunities to sell that come your way. Basically, everything you say and do when speaking with a potential client on the telephone or face to face – or when emailing them or posting material to them – is about selling who you are, how you handle your clients, how you position your coaching services and how you will add value should they decide to work with you. You may be an excellent coach, possess top-class coaching skills and be highly committed to working in ways that your clients see as adding value, but, if you don't spend time up front convincing potential clients that you are the coach they need to work with, you may not secure that much business.

WAYS YOU CAN AFFECT A POTENTIAL CLIENT'S PERCEPTION OF YOU

Consider the following four ways in which you can positively or adversely affect a potential client's perception of you.

☐ *Your tone of voice when you answer the telephone.* Do you sound preoccupied and irritated at the interruption? Do you sound open and interested that a potential new client might be calling? Can you, when the telephone rings, clear your head, pick up the receiver and focus on the train of thought of the caller? Or is half of your mind – and some of your attention – still on the work you were doing when the call came in?

☐ *The degree to which you demonstrate an accurate understanding of your potential client's stated issues.* Do you make the time to listen to a potential client's story when they first contact you? Do you seek to understand the issues that matter to them, and explore what has led them to want coaching? Can you, after having invested time in this way, clearly summarize for the potential client what you think they want to get from the coaching process and explain how working with you can help them meet those goals?

☐ *The way you describe your coaching offer.* Can you clearly and succinctly tell a potential client what they will gain from working with you? Can you describe the process and the outcomes they will experience during and after their coaching programme? Can you describe the role you'd like the potential client to play in the coaching process and tell them how you see your role as well?

☐ *The extent to which your written material is tailored to the specific potential client you are selling to.* Do you send the same written material to every potential client? Do you make sure that the written material you send to potential clients is, at least to some extent, personalized to them? Do you make sure that any written material on a proposed coaching process is bespoke and demonstrates an understanding of the specific coaching issues a potential client has previously discussed with you? If your coaching offer involves a structured process whereby clients work with you on a set number of predetermined modules, do you make sure that you also send an email or letter to your potential clients summarizing your understanding of their coaching needs, and describing how working with you will help them reach their coaching goals?

In order to buy any product or service a purchaser needs to know what they are buying, and needs to be sure that their purchase will meet their needs. One of the challenges for the new coach is to find ways of describing what they do in straightforward, simple terms that will make sense to a potential client. The added complexity for any coach – who is their own product – is that their behaviour with a potential client (verbal, non-verbal and written) is a key component of the impression they will make with that person, and is therefore a key influencer in the mind of the potential client about whether or not to work with that particular coach.

DESCRIBING STRUCTURED COACHING PROCESSES

Some of you reading this may be offering a structured coaching process to your clients, one that involves you in taking them through a predetermined number of coaching meetings, each of a set length of time. Your structured coaching process may be face to face or telephone-based. If this is the case, you may be thinking that the type of coaching you are offering means that the onus is not on you to sell yourself to your potential clients. You may be thinking that the coaching structure itself is the thing that you need to sell, and the thing that will attract clients to you. Consequently, you may consider that you are not the product in the way that I have been describing, and that the opening paragraphs of this chapter don't really apply to you. Rather you may think of yourself as simply a facilitator between the material and the potential client.

I would urge you strongly to think again. Yes, you are the facilitator of the material, very much so, and your role is to make the set material as relevant as possible to each and every client. But you are still the product you are selling as much as the process is, and, in that sense, the responsibility for selling yourself and regarding yourself as a product remains firmly with you. Clients have to want to work with *you* on the material you are qualified to coach with, as opposed to someone else. Whatever the merits of your structured material, it is still *you* that the client will be self-disclosing to, discussing that material with and revealing themselves to. It is you they will be expecting to help them reach their coaching goals.

Describing your coaching offer

Take a minute to consider all the possible different coaching niches: executive coaching, team coaching, life coaching, performance coaching, board-level coaching, solutions-focused coaching, personal coaching, career coaching and business coaching. This is not an exhaustive list, but it gives you some idea of how full the overall coaching marketplace is and how confusing it can be for a potential client to decide which type of coaching to choose let alone which specific coach to work with.

Your first job is to make these decisions easier for your potential clients. Your starting point is to have clarity in your own mind about what kind of coaching you are going to offer. So, let's start with how you are going to describe your coaching offer in terms that are simple, clear and direct, and, crucially, that tell any potential client what outcomes they can expect from working with you.

Your first task is to decide what type of coaching you are going to offer. The key issue before you is: how are you going to describe your coaching services to your potential clients? Let's break this down into smaller questions.

Consider each of the following questions which focus on how you are going to describe your coaching offer. You might like to jot down your answers in the space below each question. In describing your coaching offer to your potential clients, what do you want to say about:

The coaching process your clients will be involved in?

The outcomes they will experience at the end of the programme?

❛ *General topics that you will cover during the coaching process?* ❜

❛ *The specific coaching goals that your client wants to attain?* ❜

❛ *Your role as coach during the process?* ❜

The role your client plays during the process?

Anything else that it is important for you to include in your description of your coaching services?

SUMMARIZING YOUR COACHING OFFER

You might like to look back at what you have written below each of the questions, and experiment with writing out a paragraph that includes the key points you want to make. You can use the space below to record your ideas, or use a separate notebook.

You should now at least have a starting point for how you want to describe your coaching services. So let's consider what is perhaps the most important point of all: what your description of your coaching offer might sound like to clients.

HANDLING AN INITIAL CLIENT ENQUIRY

Consider the following two descriptions of bespoke coaching services that a potential client received from two different coaches. In each case the potential client rang the coach and asked him to answer the question: 'If I hire you as a coach, what will the coaching process involve?'

☐ *The first coach replied: 'Taking part in a coaching programme with me will involve you in six two-hour meetings, scheduled one to two weeks apart. The content and process for each of these meetings will be agreed with you in advance, depending on your coaching goals and priorities. I would like to sit down with you for at least an hour before we agree to work together and explore firstly, the context for your decision to seek out a coach; and secondly, what you'd like to achieve by working with a coach. Following that meeting I'll put together a programme outline highlighting the content and process for each of the meetings and send you a copy. Then we'll take it from there.'*

☐ *The second coach replied: 'Working with me on a coaching programme will involve you in an open-ended contract, in which we work together to evolve a programme that meets your developing needs. We'll start with where you are now, and go on to examine what you'd like to do differently and better, before developing an action plan to help you achieve those goals. If at any point you want to stop the work you are free to do so.'*

These two descriptions of coaching services accentuate completely different things. The first highlights a set number of scheduled meetings and describes the proposed coaching structure in very clear, specific detail. This presentation removes all ambiguity from the coaching offer: the potential client knows exactly what is being offered, in what order and in what way. She can see that the coach is prepared to put in time upfront to understand what she needs and wants, and that he is making a written commitment about what the programme will entail. However, once the programme commences there doesn't seem to be much room for changes of direction or process. This may deter some potential clients, especially those who would like the opportunity to bring to the table new issues that may arise as a result of a previous coaching input. However, other potential clients may be comfortable with the certainty offered by this way of working, and will therefore enjoy the confidence that this clarity brings to the coaching process.

The second description is a very different proposition. It leaves room for manoeuvre on the part of the coach, and also leaves room for changes of direction by the potential client or the coach. In this case, the client only knows where the process will start and that it will evolve to somewhere else. However, she doesn't know how long it will take to get there or by what route. She can ascertain that she will be working with a very flexible coach, one who recognizes that coaching processes may lead his clients down unexpected routes, and one who is prepared to take these detours to offer his clients best value. But the lack of certainty about the parameters and time commitment involved in this way of working may put off some potential clients, as they won't know what they are letting themselves in for. Alternatively it may suit other potential clients very well, especially those who want to explore and experiment and, to some extent, see what opportunities the coaching process creates for them.

These are two very different coaching offers. They represent different processes, values and opportunities for both potential clients and for coaches. The issue for you is to decide what you want to offer and how best to describe it so that it makes sense to clients. Do you want to offer one way of working to all your clients (as in the first example) or a variety of options from which you can select depending on what you think each client needs? If you want to offer just one way of working, do you favour the open-ended approach or the tightly structured approach? Or would you like to offer clients a mixture of a part-structured and part-evolutionary coaching process? Describing your offer in clear terms which make it accessible and valuable to potential clients is key. There are many potential clients out there who, between them, will be open to working in a variety of different ways. Your challenge is to find a way of working that appeals to these potential clients, that brings the best out of you and that you can easily describe.

Structuring your coaching offer

Having decided how to define your coaching offer, it is now time to turn your attention to how you will structure your coaching processes. If you are qualified to take clients through a structured coaching process you will already have your structure in place: a set number of coaching meetings scheduled at regular intervals. If you design and deliver bespoke coaching processes you will need to decide what structure you want to use for each client. In part, these decisions will be made on the basis of what your client's coaching goals involve and how much time they have available to work with you in any weekly or fortnightly period. For instance, a client who wants coaching on how to handle conflict and disagreement more productively is likely to need less input and a different coaching structure than a client who wants to learn about their personality, their behavioural style and how to work effectively with a range of people who have different values to their own. A client who wants to make significant progress in a relatively short period of time may need a number of closely scheduled meetings, while a client who prefers to receive some input, digest it, apply it and then come back for more may want to spread out their coaching meetings over a longer period of time. However, regardless of the length and scope of a coaching process it will be benefit from including:

- ☐ a goal-setting phase in which the coach and client can clarify the client's coaching goals;

- ☐ a data collection or research phase to explore, in detail, the issues facing the client in relation to these goals;

- ☐ an input phase in which the coach can introduce the client to coaching material that offers new insights, information, frameworks and questionnaire-based data, or to case studies that can encourage the client to see their situation and behaviour in a new light;

- ☐ an assimilation stage in which the coach and client can work together to define new behaviours, actions and thought processes that the client could usefully adopt;

- ☐ an action planning phase in which the client can choose to commit to doing things differently and better, and report back to the coach on their progress;

☐ a reporting phase in which the client can feed back to their coach any unresolved issues arising out of their new approaches and receive further input if necessary.

Differentiating your coaching offer

Remember, you are the key differentiator of your coaching offer. It is you that clients will want to work with, you who will be speaking with them. It is what you say, how you structure the coaching programmes and how you handle the issues that a client wants to talk with you about that will attract clients to you. In seeking to build a client base and grow your business, you are the one key differentiating factor that will cause a potential client to want to work with you as opposed to another coach. From the very first time they speak with you, a potential client will be assessing what they think of you, deciding how comfortable they are with you, and determining to what extent they think you will be an effective coach for them. Your material, your description of what you do as a coach, your ability to help a client define their coaching needs and goals, your coaching structure and, in some cases, your experience and qualifications will all play a part in whether or not a client chooses to work with you as opposed to someone else. But the key thing any potential client will look for is how you treat them. Specifically, they are likely to evaluate you on your ability to:

☐ engage them and set them at ease;

☐ make them feel comfortable;

☐ help them open up and talk openly about the issues they want to work with a coach on;

☐ listen to them and recognize how their experience has led to them to where they are;

☐ help them find ways of making progress towards their coaching goals;

☐ apply your knowledge to their unique life and circumstances.

The quality of relationship that you build with each of your clients will, to some extent, determine how open, safe, trusting and honest each of them is prepared to be with you. A client who feels judged, pigeon-holed, demeaned or embarrassed is unlikely to want to be open with a coach, let alone engage with the coaching process. Indeed, for some clients who are unused to talking openly about themselves, it may only take a single instance of them feeling judged for them to shut down at least part of themselves from their coach. In this case – although outwardly the coaching conversation continues and may still involve input from both the coach and the client

– on a deeper level, the client has effectively opted out of the conversation and is therefore likely to be less fully engaged than they were. Even for the most experienced and skilful coaches – those who will recognize that this has happened and want to do something about it – this can be very difficult and, in some cases, it may be impossible for a coach to build enough bridges to enable such a client to feel sufficiently comfortable to risk opening up again.

Defining your niche

If you do a web search on the words 'coaching programmes' you will find that Google lists hundreds and hundreds of websites describing different kinds of coaching services. The coaching niches listed earlier in the chapter are simply the most common ones, and you may decide that your coaching offer sits very comfortably within one of them. For instance, my own coaching offer is very much aimed at the executive coaching market. I work with senior managers and leaders, mainly, although not exclusively, in banks and professional services firms, and the aim of my work is to improve the performance of each of the clients I work with.

Your task is to decide which niche you want to use to describe your services, or if you'd prefer not to describe your coaching offer in terms of a niche at all. The point of referring to a coaching niche is to provide clarity for potential clients about what kind of coaching you are offering and, therefore, whether or not it is the right coaching for them to choose. If you decide that you don't have one tightly defined coaching market that you'd like to work in – say, for example, the executive coaching or career coaching markets – you may decide that, when you are talking about your coaching business with clients, you won't refer to a niche at all. In this case, you can simply describe your services as coaching and focus on what you do, how you work, how you provide value for clients and what kinds of outcomes they can expect from working with you.

SUMMARY

This chapter has discussed your pivotal role in the decision that any client will make about whether or not to work with you. It has hopefully encouraged you to think about all the possible ways in which you have influence over whether or not a client works with you. The chapter has also highlighted some of the choices you have about how you structure your coaching offer and define your coaching niche. Let's now go on to consider a central aspect of how you run your business: managing yourself.

3
MANAGING YOURSELF

Managing yourself is one of the three central aspects of starting and running a coaching business – the others being selling and marketing effectively, and working productively with clients – and it is absolutely crucial that you learn to do it well. Coaches who are disciplined and diligent at managing themselves will tend to make effective use of their time at work, will in the main enjoy the work–life balance they have chosen and usually have the energy they require to meet the constant challenges of running their own business. However, those who find it a struggle to manage themselves, their time, their energy and their emotions can find the roller-coaster of small business life uncomfortable, and as a consequence may not enjoy the ride often enough. The key is self-awareness. The more self-aware you are, the more likely you are to:

☐ learn from your experiences and make active choices about what to do differently and better in future;

☐ commit to the work–life balance you need to enable you to perform at your best;

☐ reach your business goals by delivering the quality and quantity of effective coaching programmes that both you and your clients want.

This chapter will focus on how to manage yourself, your time, your anxieties, your fears and your schedule. It will provide you with tips and practical ideas on remaining disciplined, focused and effective when working from home – and working largely on your own – so that your energy can go mainly towards what you need to do best: finding clients to work with and giving them best value.

Working from home

Many independent coaches work from home. They have a home office and, when not working with clients at their office, they 'go to work' at home. The upsides to this way of working are that a coach does not spend their time and money commuting to and from a place of work on a daily basis, doesn't have to pay rent on office space or buy office space outright, and doesn't have to lose valuable time to those workplace colleagues who need to talk to them. Yet there are downsides to all this, noticeably the challenges presented by not having anyone to bounce ideas off, get another perspective from or check out perceptions with, as well as the difficulty that some home-based coaches can have in making a distinction between their home life and work life when both are located in the same building.

COMMON PROBLEMS WITH WORKING FROM HOME

Three of the common struggles that coaches working from home wrestle with are the:

☐ reality that they spend quite a lot of time alone on those days when they aren't selling or working with clients;

☐ cycles of anxiety and self-doubt that they can find themselves in when faced with a perceived failure or a piece of negative feedback from a client – and the challenge of finding someone to talk such issues through with;

☐ need to stay focused while working at home with all its potential distractions.

The temptation to have a beer in the garden on a sunny day, to watch a lunchtime news bulletin, to listen to a piece of music, to walk the dog or simply to enjoy the luxury of relaxing at home during normal working hours can all result in guilt, lost time and self-recrimination. Having the option to do any of these things is part of the joy of running your own business, and in and of themselves, treating yourself to any of these activities during normal working hours should not be a problem.

The question is whether or not walking the dog or listening to music helps you to refocus more effectively on your work when you've finished the activity. Those of you moving from employment into self-employment will remember how going to chat to a colleague could enable you to refocus better on a problem or decision after the conversation: in the same way listening to music or taking a breather in the garden can help an independent coach to be more productive when they return to work. If you find that taking a few minutes out can help you refocus after you've gone back to your desk, you could usefully build these times into your usual daily routine. But if taking a breather results in you finding it more difficult to re-engage with your work when you return to your desk – or, in extreme cases, results in you not wanting to work at all – you may need to rein yourself in and keep these activities solely for your time outside work.

Structuring your working day

When you first make the transition from employment to self-employment – and from travelling to work in an office to 'going to work' in a home office – you may find yourself needing to adjust to going from a highly structured day to having a total licence in this area. Many new independent coaches will be used to the routine of travelling to their previous employer's office, or a client's premises, and working until they travel home again. This way of working creates a clear delineation for them between their work time and workplace responsibilities and their free time for socializing, pursuing hobbies, eating, sleeping and managing their household.

Becoming self-employed, and working from home, can radically change this way of thinking. New coaches can feel guilty if they take time off during the day, especially if their partner is also working and they know that he or she is still hard at it. Equally, some new coaches can find it a difficult to stop work before their usual employed leaving time even if they could, on any one day, conveniently cease working a little earlier than normal.

Some coaches can also struggle to make a clear distinction between 'work' and 'not work' in their homes. They find it difficult to switch off mentally at the end of the day, because their office is part of their home. They also struggle to shut the office door and leave work behind, or find that they go into their office at weekends and never really have a clear two-day break.

As your business grows, you may find it more difficult mentally to leave work behind you at the end of each day. You may find yourself becoming reluctant to take holidays in case you lose business. You might get into the habit of going into your office each evening to make sure you haven't forgotten to do something important. You may start downloading emails last thing at night. These tendencies can became more pronounced when you come to the end of a project and start to look for further business opportunities. If they do, and they annoy you, take a step back and assess what it is you want from your work–life balance. If you want to work when you are at work, and stop work at the end of the day, you may need to exercise greater self-discipline in making and keeping a clear distinction between 'work' and 'not work' at home.

My experience is that, no matter how motivated you are to work as a coach and run your own business, it can take time to find a way of doing so that is comfortable and effective for you. This is especially true if you are used to a structured day, are now working from a home office and are still learning about how to work effectively as a coach with new clients, new business challenges and new ways of working. If you are struggling to get the structure of your day right for you, and find yourself pulled in all sorts of directions at once, you might need to take some time out to think through how you handle this. Let's consider some of the issues you may be facing.

Managing your time

The key here is to prioritize all the items on your 'To Do' list in terms of which ones will make the most difference to your clients. Not to you, or to your accountant, or to your bank manager – not that these people aren't important – but to your clients. These are the main focus, the top priority that need your undivided attention first because they directly affect your clients' perceptions of your business. You still need to put effort into paying your suppliers on time and keeping your expense receipts in some sort of order rather than in a pile on the windowsill. However, your clients are the people who keep you in business and without them you won't have an income. They are the most important part of your business, so if you find your time is stretched:

☐ prioritize working on any improvements you need to make to your marketing material above putting shelves up in your office;

☐ prioritize making a call to a client, after a coaching meeting, before you call the manager of the venue you used for the coaching meeting to give feedback on how you were unhappy with the service;

☐ prioritize meeting a client to see what else you can do for them, and to keep in touch with their developing needs, before you meet with the person you might hire to maintain your technology system.

You will always have competing demands on your time. It's inevitable. The rule of thumb that will keep your focus in the right place (i.e. with clients and what they need from you) is to prioritize client-facing activity over and above in-house maintenance activity when you don't have time to do both. All your in-house activity (e.g. invoicing, technology maintenance, records and book-keeping, your own learning and ongoing professional development, networking with other coaches) is vital work that plays a part in the life of your business. But, there is little point in having immaculate books and insufficient income. You will find your own balance, but, every time your 'To Do' list is getting too long, step back, take a look at what is on it, and prioritize the client-facing activity over anything else. That way you can maintain your focus on the one set of business relationships you cannot afford to neglect: those with your clients and potential clients.

Feeling overwhelmed

I think that everyone running a small business is likely to run the risk of feeling overwhelmed from time to time. Why? Because it is so easy to:

☐ over-commit your time;

☐ find you have too many people to attend to and too little support for yourself;

☐ discover that, no matter how carefully you have planned and prioritized, you still have too much to do;

☐ have no one – or too few people – to speak with about challenging issues, and which, without someone else's input, you might not know how to approach with any confidence;

☐ feel that there is too much to do and too little time to do it in.

When you start to feel like this – and you are likely to at some point – stop and take stock. Make a list of all the things you need to do. Prioritize your client-facing issues. Then further prioritize the items on your list in terms of their urgency and importance. Make a plan and follow it. When you start to tackle your list, take it one item at a time and keep going – you will reach the end. When you have regained your equilibrium, sit down and purposefully review what happened to make you feel like this. Ask yourself:

☐ 'At what point did I start to feel overwhelmed?'

☐ 'What specific issues contributed to this feeling?'

☐ 'What can I do to make sure I don't end up there again?'

In regularly reviewing your performance, and purposefully learning from your experiences, you can make sure that you learn and grow as your business does, and that you don't make the same mistakes twice. It's inevitable that as a sole practitioner with a growing business you will, from time to time, have too much on your plate. However, there will be trigger points that you can learn to spot in advance. Knowing what they are will enable you to take steps to pre-empt some of the discomfort you'll go through if you get so overwhelmed that you don't know which way to turn.

Managing your activity

You may have bags of energy and resolve for, variously, gaining a coaching qualification, getting your marketing material together, networking with other coaches and attending new business start up conferences or workshops. However, the background from which many coaches move into the profession quite often does not include extensive sales experience. So when it comes to actually contacting potential clients, new coaches can find all sorts of irrelevant but pressing issues to attend to. They stall. The step of actually contacting clients can be a daunting one. The fear of saying the wrong thing to a potential client and putting them off can leave some new coaches unable to take that first step. Other coaches may just not know how to get started and will get caught up in a lot of planning but not much action.

WHAT PREVENTS YOU FROM SELLING?

You might like to consider the following scenarios. Which of them, or which combination of them, do you most identify with?

☐ *You are concerned that, no matter how much planning you do, you'll never be ready enough to speak with a potential client. You want to plan so thoroughly that you will be prepared for any sales eventuality and any question that your potential client may throw at you. Fear of being insufficiently complete and therefore unable to respond adequately to a potential client when you really need to make a good impression keeps you from selling to them.*

☐ *You are concerned that, with so many opportunities out there, you'll miss the boat. You spend a lot of time in vigorous, but slightly haphazard, activity — promoting your services, initiating meetings, creating and exploring potential new sales opportunities and business relationships. However, you are now running the risk of not completing anything you've started properly. Fear of missing out on something important means that you've taken on too much and, potentially, will miss out on some opportunities because you've spread yourself too thinly.*

☐ *One of your key motivators in deciding to become a coach is to help others and make a valued contribution to their lives. You are used to being part of a team at work and, in this respect, you enjoy and need to be in supportive workplace relationships. You are finding the isolation of working as an independent coach rather disabling. Rather than giving you the room to do things your way that you envisaged it would, the autonomy you now have is actually inhibiting you from taking independent action. You just cannot decide, commit and get on with it. You spend a lot of time reflecting on what you could do and networking with other coaches; you've attended a lot of personal development seminars but you don't seem able to take that extra step and start to sell your coaching business. You are getting frustrated with yourself and discouraged.*

☐ *Since deciding to set up in business as a coach, you've made many excellent contacts and have thoroughly enjoyed meeting potential clients, other coaches and new business associates. However, having made so much headway you are now struggling to bring any of your possible projects to fruition. You have various selling and marketing documents at differing stages of incompletion; you haven't planned enough and don't have any clearly defined goals to work towards, which makes prioritizing difficult. You are getting pulled in different directions simultaneously due to your enthusiasm for yet another more interesting contact or potentially exciting opportunity that comes along. You are now concerned that the very strength you have – going out there and making contacts – is turning into a weakness as you keep making more new contacts but struggle to follow through adequately with any of them.*

Getting the balance right

These four scenarios are designed to illustrate how good intentions and your areas of strength can become weaknesses if you fail to manage yourself effectively. This clearly requires a balance. You need to be able to attend to each of the following four sets of activities without concentrating too much on any one of them and consequently neglecting the others.

☐ Set realistic goals for yourself and work steadily towards them. You might want to break each project up into smaller pieces of work and allocate a specific day or more in your diary for accomplishing each one. This way you will see yourself getting through the work piece by piece, and won't be tempted to try to complete everything at once, thereby exhausting yourself in a matter of days. You will also be able to look ahead in your diary, see when you have space coming up for further selling and marketing activities, and plan in advance what you need to do and when you will have the time to do it.

☐ Plan and prepare in a detailed and methodical way so that you give yourself the best chance of reaching your goals. You might want to make a comprehensive list at the start of each project detailing absolutely everything that you need to do to complete it to your satisfaction. You can then make sure that you allocate a date in your diary to each of these tasks, as described above. This will save you relying on your memory and expending energy worrying that you've already forgotten to do something by a specific date or that you might forget something in the future.

☐ Establish and maintain effective peer relationships with other coaches and business contacts, while still deciding for yourself what you are going to do. Before meeting with a peer contact to talk about any of the issues you face as an independent coach, make sure that you have thought about any potential steps you could take to resolve an issue and go to the peer meeting prepared to speak about them. Use that meeting to explore your potential solutions and improve them, rather than to outline problems and look for direction in how to tackle them.

□ Make new contacts and be open to exploring novel and interesting new ideas, while prioritizing which to follow up immediately and which later on, depending on your current goals. You might want to keep up to date with interesting contacts who you are not currently working with on a cyclical basis, perhaps making a diary note to contact a few people at every month end or at the start of every month.

Managing your energy

It is vital that you use your energy wisely. If you have moved from employment into independent coaching you are probably used to having colleagues around to handle many of the key functions of business: finance, selling, marketing, technology, administration and/or office supplies. You will be in a situation where you alone are responsible for all of these aspects of running your business and, if you are not careful, you could end up spending so much energy on maintaining your business that you haven't got enough left to spend on working with clients.

Learning to manage your energy is vital. You need to work within your limits and make sure that you build into your working week sufficient replenishing activities that you don't become over-tired on a regular basis. You need to ask yourself:

□ 'Where do I get my energy from?'

□ 'What drains me?'

□ 'How do I replenish my energy?'

Consider the following two sets of bullet points, which you may recognize as being based on Myers-Briggs Type Indicator theory. Do you relate more strongly to the statements in the first box or the second? Or do you see bits of yourself in both?

■ You enjoy working alone, find it easy to spend several hours focusing steadily on one thing and, when in this mode, find telephone calls and other interruptions disruptive.

■ If you spend all day being with people you prefer some quiet time in the evening to re-charge your batteries.

■ You are comfortable responding in workplace relationships and, at times, could do with being a bit more communicative.

■ After giving a presentation – a quite draining activity for you – you prefer to have some downtime to recover. You find all-day back-to-back meetings leave you feeling drained.

■ You give your best contributions at meetings when you've had a chance to think through the issues beforehand.

- You find that if you spend too much time alone you get fractious and bored. When this happens you need to pick up the phone and speak to someone, or go out and talk to a business contact.
- You enjoy spending the day working with people and think that discussing ideas, debating issues and talking things through is the best way to make progress on them.
- You don't get drained by spending all day with people. In fact it energises you. You need the spark that being with other people provides you with, and you use discussions to make decisions and come to conclusions.
- You prefer to talk to someone than to write your ideas down. You like to take the initiative in workplace relationships and, at times, could do with speaking less and listening more.
- You can easily spend all day with people and still find the energy to go out in the evenings too.

If you relate more strongly to the statements in the first box you are likely to get your energy from solitude and reflection. You will keep your energy levels high by purposefully scheduling time alone in your diary two or three times a week. Make these 'meetings with yourself' as much of a priority as your meetings with clients or potential clients.

If you relate more strongly to the statements in the second box you are likely to get your energy from interacting with people and being around them. You will keep your energy banks recharged by arranging meetings with other people on those days when you know you will otherwise be alone in your office all day. Plan ahead and organize yourself to meet with network contacts or your supervisor (see Chapter 6) at lunchtime or the early afternoon. Just having that date in your diary will help you remain focused when working alone because you will know that a conversation with someone else is scheduled for later in the day.

Being the sole decision maker and problem solver

Many coaches find being the sole decision maker and problem solver in their business liberating. They can simply decide what to do and go out and do it, without having to invest time and energy in influencing other people before taking action. However, whether or not you are excited by the prospect of autonomy, it makes sense to take stock of your strengths and weaknesses as a decision maker and problem solver.

Knowing what issues you are likely to focus on, and those which you are likely to overlook, can be vital if you are to make well-rounded, effective decisions and find workable solutions to the problems you want to tackle. Finding business contacts with opposite strengths to your own, and deliberately talking through the issues with them before you make important decisions, can be an effective way of making sure you have considered every angle before you take action. It can be a challenge to find appropriate coaching colleagues to speak openly with (see Chapter 8), but it is important that you find at least one trustworthy person with whom you can talk and from whom you can get another perspective.

Rewarding yourself

If you are coming to coaching from a results and reward orientated employer you may be struggling with the issue of: 'How *do* I reward myself? And for what?' It is a truism to say that you can't pay yourself anything if your business doesn't have enough income to support paying you. But assuming it does, and that you're planning to pay yourself a regular monthly income, how are you going to incentivize or reward your performance thereafter?

You can decide to pay yourself a sales bonus, or a delivery bonus, based on meeting predetermined targets you've set yourself. You can treat yourself whenever you've sold a coaching programme or performed in a way that you believe deserves recognition. You can keep written records of all the praise and positive feedback you've been given by clients and review it at regular intervals. You can pat yourself on the back and say 'well done' when you've delivered a coaching programme that a client was pleased with. But, at the end of the day, no colleague or peer or boss is going to say to you 'you did a good job today'. You need to find ways of doing this for yourself.

If you see reward and recognition primarily in financial terms, you may want to set yourself targets against which you will award yourself a bonus. In this case you could incentivize yourself for income generation, or for the volume of referral business you get, or for the number of new clients you secure in any given period. Alternatively, you may decide to incentivize other aspects of running your business instead of these more obvious ones. The choice is yours. But in making that choice, you need to make sure it is something that motivates *you*. You may see reward and recognition in terms that are other than financial. If so you may decide instead to award yourself in other ways, such as an extra day off in lieu of meeting selling or delivery targets. The point of a reward is that it should be something you enjoy, so select those rewards that mean something to you, that will encourage you to give of your best and that you'll enjoy when you award them to yourself.

Taking time off/scheduling holidays

This simply has to be done. You must take time off. You must schedule holidays and take them. The role of coach will involve you in a series of business relationships where you must make yourself available to your clients by listening to them, hearing what they are saying and providing input to help them move towards their coaching goals. This is potentially exciting and enriching work – but it is also potentially draining work which can create high wear-and-tear on you if you don't take sufficient time off. The drain placed on you of securing business and delivering it, looking for more business to deliver and delivering that, can result one day in you realizing that you are over-tired, something you had not recognized early enough to pre-empt. Many coaches find that they have to make it a priority to listen to that small voice inside them that tells them they are doing too much and need to rest. This voice can easily be drowned out. After all, if you take time off or choose to take things slower, there won't be anyone else to do the tasks you don't do.

If you are getting over-extended, stop now. Getting over-tired can mean that it takes you longer to recover than if you don't get that tired in the first place. Regular, shorter holidays are a good idea because you don't run the risk of losing business through being unavailable for a fortnight or a month. And, you can still get recharged and leave the responsibility of your business behind for a few days.

Staying focused

Working as a coach is a brilliant job. It is rewarding and challenging, satisfying and enriching. The role of coach can enable you to:

☐ establish and enjoy ongoing relationships with your clients;

☐ meet new people, clients and business contacts on a regular basis;

☐ learn new things from a great many of these people;

☐ have the satisfaction of knowing that you are helping other people every day you go to work;

☐ have opportunities for constant learning and growth for yourself;

☐ have the freedom to decide who to work with and in what way;

☐ enjoy more autonomy and independence than most people have at work;

☐ have the option to manage your time as you choose;

☐ have the option to schedule and take time off to suit your needs.

Keep your eye on these benefits and work steadily towards them, especially when things are tough, tiring or lonely. If they aren't enough to keep your mind focused on the tasks in hand, what will be?

SUMMARY

In this chapter we have examined what you need to do to manage yourself effectively. Let's now move on to consider how you are going to sell and market your coaching business.

4
SELLING AND MARKETING YOUR BUSINESS

It is vital that you sell and market your business. Simply put, it is something to which you must devote dedicated, planned time on an ongoing basis. You cannot work any other way. Working as a sole practitioner means that you are likely to be the only person delivering coaching meetings in your business, the only person handling the day-to-day management of your business and the only person going out there and looking for new business. You need to devote planned time to all three aspects of your practice, and this means that you need to sell and market as a regular, planned part of your usual working routine.

Some new coaches really enjoy this side of their business. As a result they are:

☐ excited by the prospect of finding new and interesting ways to describe what they do as a coach;

☐ energized by the new people they meet and the interesting conversations they have with potential clients;

☐ invigorated by the challenge of getting out there and telling people about what they are doing.

Other coaches will find the need to sell and market a constant strain – a stressful part of their job that they need to make themselves attend to and psych themselves up for. Selling activity drains their energy: they don't enjoy it, but they do see it as a necessary part of running a business. They can usually recognize that if they don't sell they won't earn, so they will still work hard at applying themselves and learning effective selling and marketing skills.

Whether you are looking forward to this aspect of running your coaching business, or whether you are just hoping you'll get through it, this chapter is for you. It will examine the various options you have for selling and marketing. The chapter will examine how and where to market and sell your services, what to say when you do sell and market, how to make the most of the selling and marketing opportunities you create, how much you should charge and whether or not to use a website and/or other promotional materials. It will also examine how best to ask existing clients for referrals, whether or not to develop a mission statement and whether or not to work as an associate coach. By the end of it you should be clear about what you want from your selling and marketing activity, and know which areas of selling and marketing activity to focus on to bring about the outcomes that you want.

What does 'selling and marketing your business' mean to you?

For the purposes of this chapter I'd like to introduce an uncomplicated set of definitions which may seem simplistic to specialists but will serve our needs here. I'd like to use the term 'selling' to refer to any conversation you have with a potential client or existing client in order to promote your business. This definition includes telephone calls, conference calls, one-to-one face-to-face conversations, face-to-face group meetings and more formal presentations when you talk about what you do as a coach with the intention of gaining new business. I'd like to use the term 'marketing' to refer to all the materials that support this activity: your website, flyers, brochures, emailed information, advertisements, business cards and so on.

First of all I'd like you to step back for a minute and focus on what the phrase 'selling and marketing your business' conjures up for you. You might like to close your eyes as you do this, and then use the space below to jot down any words, phrases or images that come into your mind.

You might now like to circle the three or four words from the following list that best describe what you feel when you consider the phrase 'selling and marketing your business'. If none of these words accurately describes your feelings feel free to add your own words in the space below them:

Excited	Alone	Bold	Glum
Dismayed	Energised	Apprehensive	Indifferent
Curious	Interested	Determined	Isolated
Influential	Unsure	Reticent	Capable
Afraid	Optimistic	Calm	Overwhelmed

Look back at what you have written and the words you have chosen. What picture do they paint? Perhaps one that shows someone who is up for selling and marketing activity and is looking forward to it? You might see selling and marketing activity as an exciting prospect, one that will lead to you towards:

☐ successfully promoting your new business venture;

☐ meeting new and interesting people, some of whom will become clients.

But then again, perhaps the words you've chosen paint an alternative picture of someone who has concerns and anxieties about selling and marketing? You might see selling and marketing activity as a daunting and scary prospect, one that could lead to:

☐ the failure of your plans to run your own coaching business;

☐ you feeling exposed and humiliated.

Or perhaps the words you've chosen paint a picture somewhere in between? You might see selling and marketing activity as something you have to get on and do because without it your business simply won't get off the ground, but it's something that you are going to have to make yourself do rather than something you are keen to engage with.

The prospect of selling and marketing

If you regard the prospect of selling and marketing your business with something approaching buoyant enthusiasm you will be well placed to harness your optimism and put it to good use in the sales process. The challenge will be not to let your natural openness to selling and marketing lull you into a false sense of security. You will still need to develop top notch face-to-face selling skills and produce first-class marketing material to make the most of what you've got. Don't be tempted to 'wing it'. You will still need to prepare for, practise and evaluate your sales presentations, even if you don't feel that this is necessary.

If, on the other hand, you view the prospect of selling and marketing your business with something approaching dismay you will need to acknowledge that this really is how you feel – and then still go out there and do it anyway. Learning to sell – by honing your selling skills until they are first class – and learning to produce excellent marketing materials will enable you to re-evaluate how you feel about these activities once you have positive experiences to draw on. Feeling uncomfortable about selling and marketing, and yet being competent at both of these activities is a perfectly compatible situation. Don't let your present discomfort lead you to believe that you can't learn to sell and market effectively. You can. Once you are a practised and skilled seller and marketer of your coaching services you will feel less apprehensive about future selling and marketing opportunities.

The remainder of this chapter will be devoted to taking you through a process to help you to decide how best to sell and market your business. To begin with it will focus on selling activity, then move on to marketing activity, and it will end with a discussion of other sales- and marketing-related issues.

Your approach to selling

Everyone sells in a different way: there is no 'right' or 'wrong' to it. However, there are some important principles which can help you sell effectively. A key set of these is based around knowing your own selling style and adapting it to suit the varied needs and requirements of the different people you will be selling to. Later on in the chapter I'll take you through how to read potential clients' styles, but for now let's focus on your personal selling style.

As you read this, you may or may not have had any experience of one-to-one selling conversations with potential clients. Those of you who have already begun to sell your business you might like to read the following cameos with one of those experiences in mind. Those of you who haven't yet begun to sell your business you might like to take a look at them with your natural workplace style in mind instead. These cameos are derived from behavioural styles theories.

IDENTIFYING YOUR SELLING STYLE

❛ *Which of the following selling styles, or which combination of the selling styles, can you most identify with?*

☐ *You are goal-orientated, factual and logical in the way you approach selling (or your work). You enjoy, and may even actively seek out, a challenge. When describing your coaching programmes (or your work) you like to emphasize the bigger picture and the outcomes that your clients (or your business contacts) will benefit from. You enjoy being able to create a structure for your coaching programmes (or work) that enables those outcomes to be achieved efficiently and effectively. You like to clarify direction and generate momentum in a sales (or workplace) conversation. You get worried if you think that you are going to miss a sales (or work) opportunity or fail to take full advantage of the situation. You find it stressful if you are in a position where you can't influence key sales (or workplace) decisions effectively. You sell by generating and conveying excitement for your ideas and approach: an obvious enthusiasm which causes other people to want to work with you.*

☐ *You are goal-orientated, methodical, structured and careful in the way you approach selling (or your work). You rarely make factual errors and, when you describe your coaching programmes (or your work), you like to provide your rationale as well as plenty of detail about what you are proposing. You think it important that you devote time to upfront planning for a coaching programme (or workplace project). This way you can ensure quality outcomes and avoid errors. You are at your best when you can make a full and comprehensive coaching (or work) plan and then follow it. You are data-centred in your approach to selling (or work) and dislike being in a situation where you have insufficient information about what a potential client (or project) requires. In these cases you find it difficult to make decisions about the details of a coaching programme (or workplace project). You prefer to be thoroughly prepared and find it stressful if you are expected to move ahead with a sales (or workplace) conversation before you have enough background information. You sell by creating a persuasive, cogent, factual argument that influences people because it makes clear links between processes and outcomes.*

☐ *You are relationship-oriented and enjoy building harmonious relationships with the people to whom you are selling (or working). You enjoy building rapport with your potential clients (or workplace contacts) and are an able and supportive mentor. You are at your best when the people you are selling to (working with) are open about what they need from you and you are able to respond to those needs.*

You want your coaching programmes (or work) to make a valued contribution to the lives of your clients (or workplace contacts). You therefore emphasize what you can do for them and how your approach is both relevant and excellent. You are very committed to your coaching work (or work) and, in return, expect a high degree of participation and involvement from your clients (or workplace contacts). You find it stressful if you think that your contribution is not valued, recognized or trusted by your potential clients (or workplace contacts). You sell by conveying a personal conviction for what you believe in.

☐ *You are relationship-oriented and enjoy having influence with your clients (or workplace contacts). You enjoy bringing people together to get things done, and therefore relish the opportunity to sell your business to potential new clients. You are skilled at managing people's perceptions and marketing your achievements. You find it easy to engage potential clients (or workplace contacts) in conversation. You are naturally flexible and gregarious, and you enjoy changes of direction in a sales (or workplace) conversation. When speaking with a potential client (or workplace contact) you emphasize what the two of you can achieve together. You find it stressful if you think that you lack the influence you'd like to have with a particular client (or workplace contact). You sell by knowing instinctively how to put an argument across so that it has maximum impact with a particular person. You may therefore relate the same facts in different ways to different people in different sales conversations.*

KNOWING YOUR OWN STYLE

Knowing your own style is important because, once you know your own preferences and values, you can adjust what you say when you are selling to take into account the potentially different preferences and values of your clients. For instance, let's say you favour a combination of the second and third styles: a mixture of a methodical, fact-based, detailed approach to selling combined with a desire to build harmonious, involving and valued business relationships. Let's also say that many of the people you sell to happen to favour the first style, which involves a preference for:

☐ headlines rather than rationale;

☐ the big picture rather than the detail;

☐ hearing about outcomes rather than the process;

☐ getting things done and moving on rather than investing in relationships;

☐ punchy business conversations rather than friendly business chat.

In order to have maximum influence with your potential clients you will have to provide them with the kinds of information that they will value and not the kinds of information you'd naturally select to give them where these are different. This will mean omitting quite a lot of the detail, rationale and method about how you work – information that you'd like to give to demonstrate that you know your stuff – which, if you included it, would run you the significant risk of 'switching off' your potential client. Instead, you'll need to include bullet point headings about what the client will get from working with you, information which can highlight how you will help them and what working with you will achieve for them. If they want more detail at any stage, they'll ask you.

In order to decide how to adapt your natural style to suit the preferences of your potential clients, you will need to be able to read their styles accurately, as well as know your own. Later on in the chapter you'll find a section entitled 'Selling to the style of your potential client'. This section will help you find out how to read your potential clients' styles so you can flex your own style accordingly. But, for now, knowing your own style and its underlying values is enough. So let's go on to consider what selling is and how you can do it.

How to sell your coaching business

Selling is actually quite a simple process. No matter how you feel about it, at the end of the day, 'selling your business' is really a matter of:

☐ going out there;

☐ telling people what you do;

☐ finding out what they, or people they know, might need from you as a coach;

☐ making clear how you can meet those needs;

☐ describing the benefits of working with you to potential clients.

Remember that it is you – the product – that a client must want to work with. So the style with which you accomplish these five things is of paramount importance. Every time you speak to someone about what you do you are sowing seeds. That person may need coaching themselves, even if they hadn't realized it at the start of the conversation. Equally, they themselves may not need coaching services but people they know might well do instead. If they are impressed with your style and approach they might refer you to their contacts. View every opportunity to speak about what you do as an opportunity to sow seeds that may well, with a little nurturing, bring you business, and give you the opportunity to help new clients achieve their coaching goals. To sell effectively therefore you need to:

☐ find suitable people to sell to;

☐ describe your services accurately and concisely;

☐ listen effectively for what potential clients need and want;

☐ describe clearly and fully the outcomes and benefits to potential clients of working with you;

☐ relay this information in an engaging way.

Finding people to sell to

It is self-evident to say that you will need to find the right people to talk to when you start to sell your business. Whichever coaching niche you choose to work in, you need to target people who are:

☐ interested in development and growth;

☐ open to the possibility of working with a coach – or who know other people who might be;

☐ able to invest their time in talking with you about your coaching services and their coaching needs.

There are many, many ways of finding people to sell to: cold calling, taking a stall at a coaching and development exhibition, joining professional coaching bodies, offering taster sessions for free, asking your existing contacts for referrals or introductions and many more. You might like to consider joining a business network organization as one way of getting started. Membership of a business network will provide you with an opportunity to attend a weekly or monthly meeting where you will be able to promote your business. Members do this by listening to one another's short presentations about their businesses and then, in the following week or month, by looking out for referral opportunities for one another (see 'Useful Weblinks' at the end of this book which outlines a couple of options).

The key point here is that selling is about how you handle the person, or audience, you are speaking with *in the moment you are speaking with them*. There is no magic formula: it is you and your passion for your field that will influence potential clients to work with you. The way you structure your presentation or selling conversation matters as well, but at the end of the day, it is your ability to put across your coaching offer and make it relevant to the needs of those you are speaking with that will differentiate you from other coaches.

Everything you say about your coaching business is a form of selling activity. What you say and how you say it will result in clients and potential clients forming views about your credibility, your values as a coach, your effectiveness as a supplier of coaching services, your character and your approach. You can never be 'off duty' when you are in the company of clients or potential clients. This doesn't mean that you cannot enjoy their company, but it does mean they will always be the client and that you will always be the provider – or potential provider – of a service to them.

Talking about what you do

So, the style you adopt when you talk about what you do is all important.

DESCRIBING COACHING SERVICES

Consider the following two examples: a newly qualified coach goes to a networking meeting, excited at the opportunity to describe her coaching offer to a room full of people who might be able to make referrals for her, or who may themselves be looking for a coach. She is given five minutes to describe what she does in any way she chooses.

☐ *She spends most of the time talking about her background in order to give the audience a sense of her qualifications and experience and to justify her decision to set up as a coach. Part-way through she begins to talk about the specific issues she feels clients might want to work with her on. After five minutes she stops and refers the audience to a flyer which she has placed beneath their chairs.*

☐ *She decides to focus her presentation on the audience. She starts by asking them to spend 15 seconds thinking about and identifying a recent situation they didn't handle well. She tells them that this situation could involve a meeting with a client, a colleague, their boss, a family member or a friend. She also tells them that it might have involved them leaving the conversation thinking that they didn't have the influence they might have had, or that they hadn't got their points across well enough, or that they hadn't been listened to, or that they had been unable to put things in a way that made sense to the people with them. After giving the audience 15 seconds thinking time she asks them to stop. She waits for them to re-engage with her and then says that she regularly helps clients to replace ineffective behaviour with more effective behaviour that will help them secure the influence they want to have. She explains that her work involves a process in which she helps clients to take time out from their day-to-day lives and work to look for ways of doing things more effectively. She maintains that they don't have to work with her for long to experience real and sustained behaviour change, and tells the audience that she'll be available at the back of the room after the meeting should anyone want to discuss in further detail what she might be able do for them.*

These two sales presentations accentuate completely different things. The first one highlights the experience and background of the coach. The audience will learn a lot about her, what she has done in her previous career, why she went into coaching and what coaching means to her. Some more self-aware members of the audience may be able to make mental links between the information she then gives about her coaching work and their own situation. However, many of them won't have got far with this, or won't have been able to do so at all, within the five-minute time span. So what will audience members be able to take away from the presentation?

Most will probably have decided whether they like the coach or not, but still won't understand very much about what she could do for them personally. Others, especially those new to coaching, might not have been able to grasp what coaching is, what working with her would involve, how long the process would take or what it is for. Part of the reason for this confusion is that she didn't describe in sufficient detail what outcomes her clients could expect, and didn't adequately detail the full range of circumstances in their lives that might prompt them to come and work with her in the first place. Nor did she describe any of the processes that she used in her coaching programmes.

Will any of the audience want to engage her or refer her to their friends and contacts? Possibly, but not definitely, because the best they could say is that she seems like a nice person, but they didn't really get a sense of what she does. Indeed, a proportion of the people in the audience may well write her off by concluding that she was just starting out, didn't describe what she did clearly, lost their interest early on and seemed diffident and reluctant to engage with the audience. They might also draw unfavourable and inaccurate conclusions about her performance as a coach based on this one presentation.

What about the second presentation? This starts with the audience and continues from there as they are asked to focus on themselves and identify a real, recent experience that left them feeling they'd missed a trick. From that moment onward the coach is working with the internal agenda of each audience member in a personal process that is relevant to them. The subsequent information she gives enables each member of the audience to learn about what she does and how it will benefit them. They will learn that working with her doesn't have to take a long time, and that she will speak further with them about their issues straight after the meeting. They will also learn that, mostly, she is primarily interested in them and their issues. Will some audience members decide to speak further with her or refer her to their friends and contacts? The answer would probably be yes, because they will now have a greater understanding of what she does, why it is useful to them and what is involved, and they will also realize that she offers a client-centred *service.*

These scenarios represent two very different ways of selling coaching services and they concentrate on two different sets of issues. In the first presentation the focus is on the coach, her experience and background; in the second presentation the focus is on the audience members and their potential coaching issues. Therefore these two presentations encapsulate the different offers, values and opportunities available to potential clients. The clear principle here is that selling is about the potential client and not the coach *per se*. Of course it must be said that what the coach does, how they coach, and what processes they use and so on do matter. But primarily, the sales conversation needs to be about the client – what they need, what they require, what they want and how you as their coach can help them achieve their coaching goals. It is a real skill to be able to keep a conversation focused on a client for long enough to be able to engage them, and it is an art that has to be learned over time. The key issue for you as a coach is to practise handling such sales conversations in a relatively safe environment so that when you come to do the real thing you are on top form.

Planning your sales approach

We've covered quite a bit of ground thus far and so you might want to spend a few minutes summarizing the conclusions you've reached. The conclusions that you came to during Chapter 2, about how you want to define your coaching offer, will also be relevant here.

You might want to look back at the notes you made in that chapter before considering the following sales-orientated questions. If you wish to you can use the space below each one to jot down your answer, or if you prefer, use your own notebook.

In your sales conversations and presentations what issues do you want to focus on primarily?

What do you want to learn about your clients and potential clients?

What is the key information you want to convey to clients and potential clients during these conversations?

At the end of the sales conversation what do you want them to know about you as their potential coach?

At the end of the sales conversation what do you want them to know about your coaching programmes?

At the end of the sales conversation what do you want them to think further about before you speak with them again?

Your coaching programme outline

So far we have examined what you will want to say to clients and potential clients during a sales conversation. We've also looked at how you might want to say these things. As a next step we need to discuss the written material you will provide to your clients as part of the sales process, written material that will enable them to decide finally whether or not to work with you. This written material is your coaching programme outline.

If you are going to work with clients using a set coaching process you likely have a prepared coaching programme outline available to you already. This is the pre-printed document that tells clients what you are going to do together and in what way. Provided that you stick to the exact programme outlined in this prepared document you won't need to produce any other material that describes what you are going to do. However, if you are going to develop a bespoke or part-tailored coaching process for each of your clients, you will need to write a coaching programme outline for each one of them. Either way, it is essential to give each client a written programme outline as part of the sales process and before you commence each coaching programme. This written material needs to be specific to the coaching programme you are going to deliver for that client and, as such, it must provide details about the exact programme they are going to participate in.

The programme outline serves several purposes, the most important of which is to describe the features of the programme the client is going to work with you on, so that:

□ both you and your client are clear about what you have contracted to do together;

□ each of you has a detailed reference point for your work together so that, should you need to clarify anything about the process further down the road, you have a written outline to refer back to;

□ there can be no misunderstanding about what you are going to do and how you are going to do it;

□ your client knows in advance what to expect during the coaching programme and can be thinking about how they can contribute to the process most effectively.

□ your client can see written evidence of your understanding of their coaching needs and your plan for meeting them.

The coaching programme outline is essential to your sales process because many clients will not make up their mind about whether or not to work with you until they have seen such detailed information about a proposed programme. This is especially true in executive coaching where many of the organizations that work with executive coaches will need to see a proposal or programme outline as part of their due diligence and internal contracting processes. Writing an original programme outline for each client does take time, but the effort involved is well worth it because of the ensuing business it can create for you. If you choose to go down this route, you might like to include the following sections in your tailored coaching programme outlines.

☐ **The purpose of the coaching programme**. This is your opportunity to demonstrate to your client the depth of your understanding of their coaching needs. This section might include:
  - a description of the coaching issues that your client wants to work on;
  - the key challenges that these issues create for them in their life or work or both;
  - how the programme you propose will meet these coaching needs.

☐ **The process of the coaching programme**. This is your opportunity to outline, in as much detail as you think necessary, the process you are proposing. This section might include:
  - a description of the objectives and outcomes within each coaching meeting in the programme;
  - a description of what telephone or email support, if any, you will offer outside the scheduled coaching meetings;
  - information about how often you'd like to schedule your meetings;
  - information about where you'd like to hold your meetings.

☐ **The costs of the coaching programme**. This section must include all the costs as you know them, so that there are no surprises for your client later on. These costs might include:
  - your fees for the programme;
  - the charges you want to make for materials (e.g. any commercially-produced questionnaires that you may need to purchase for the programme);
  - the charges you anticipate making for travel and accommodation if these are appropriate.

☐ **Your client list**, or if you are just starting out, a summary of your background experience and qualifications as a coach.

☐ **Any other information** you think would be effective at demonstrating your credentials to coach this client on these issues.

☐ **Your contact details**.

Remember, the purpose of the coaching programme outline is to do the following:

☐ To provide a potential client who has yet to decide whether or not to work with you with detailed information on the process you are proposing to meet their coaching needs so that they can make up their mind about working with you.

☐ To act as a detailed summary of the programme a client has already asked you to deliver for them.

In either case, and for different reasons, the more comprehensive the coaching programme outline, and the more exact it is as a summary of what you intend, the better.

Selling to the style of your potential client

So far, we have been exploring how you might sell, both verbally and in written form. Now it's time to focus on the people you'll be selling to: your clients and potential clients. Different clients and potential clients respond to different approaches. Your first task when holding a sales conversation with anyone is to determine which style they are using, and to make sure that the description of your coaching services is relevant to the values underpinning their style, not yours.

You will recall that you will have already identified which selling style, or combination of selling styles, you naturally use. You might now like to consider the following scenarios which illustrate four different styles, or combinations of styles, that clients and potential clients might use. As you read them, you may want to keep a recent sales conversation in mind, or if you haven't yet started to sell your coaching business, you might like to refer back to a recent work conversation in which you tried to influence a workplace contact. Again, each of the four cameos is derived from behavioural styles theories.

SELLING TO YOUR CLIENT'S STYLE

☐ *Your client or potential client is interested in headline information and wants to speak with you primarily about outcomes and deliverables. He is immediate and direct, quick to make up his mind and, once convinced, will become committed to a course of action. He is goal-orientated, factual and logical. A sales conversation that focuses on what you will deliver for him, and what those* results will do for him, will serve you best when selling to him. He wants to know how you will structure the coaching programme you propose, what this structure will achieve for him, at what point he can expect to see results and what these outcomes will mean to him. He probably values autonomy and independence, and likes to be challenged. So he will be particularly interested to hear about how the coaching programme you propose will enable him to become more effective and productive, as well as the ways in which it will stretch and test him. He is likely to get impatient with too much detail at this stage of the selling process, and will be much more interested in hearing about the concept. Having understood your proposition he may ask you specific questions but, overall, he will prefer to focus the conversation on the bigger picture – what you are proposing, what it will achieve and how these outcomes will benefit him in the areas of his coaching goals. This client may be prepared to make an on-the-spot decision about whether or not to work with you, so make sure that you keep the conversation in those areas that matter to him. He doesn't want much rationale or explanation and will respond best to being given the key points.

☐ *Your client or potential client is quite risk-averse and discussing participating in a coaching programme may be something new for her. She is likely to be factual, goal-orientated, cautious and methodical. She would like to be taken through the coaching process step by step. She is good at planning and would like detail at this stage – on what the process will entail, how long it will take, what the structure of the programme will be, what she will be expected to contribute to it and what your role will be. She will appreciate a written reminder of these things so that she can consider them after the conversation with you. She is unlikely to want to make a decision then and there, but would instead like to go away and reflect on what you've said before either making a decision or deciding to speak with you again. During the conversation, this potential client is likely to want to think through what you are saying and, at these times, she will appreciate a chance to reflect on what you have said before you speak with one another again. She is thorough and rigorous and will want complete answers to all the points she puts to you. Being risk-averse, this client will respond best to an approach that emphasizes how the outcomes from the coaching programme you are proposing tie into and build on her current way of doing things. She will also want to talk through her concerns about the coaching programme in a calm and factual way, and will want you to provide meaningful rationale for ameliorating all her issues with it. The more you can demonstrate how the outcomes from the programme will extend her skills, abilities or thinking in relation to her coaching goals, the more interested she is likely to be. She is primarily data-centred and will respond well to you demonstrating your knowledge of your subject area.*

☐ *Your client or potential client is interested in growth and development. He values relationships and likes to build rapport. Ideally, he would like to work with a coach who he gets on with and will enjoy working with. He is probably both warm and open, and will respond well to a collaborative way of doing things. The sales discussion needs to demonstrate your qualities as a coach: your ability to listen, your ability to reflect back your understanding of what you have heard him say, your ability to ask insightful questions and your ability to remain supportive while challenging him. To work with you, your client must believe that participating in the coaching programme will add value to his life or work, and that this will enable him to become more of the person he wants to be in relation to his coaching goals. This client will also appreciate being involved, at least to some extent, in the decision-making processes that surround the coaching programme. He'd like to be consulted, as much as is realistic, about what the programme will focus on, in what way it will be structured, how often you'll meet and so on. Focusing the sales conversation on the ways in which the programme will help him grow in relation to his coaching goals and using the time to build a relationship with him will serve you best. This potential client may also want time to think about the programme before deciding to participate in it but, ultimately, he will be swayed by whether or not he thinks that you have the qualities he is looking for in a coach.*

☐ *Your client or potential client sees herself as an influential person, someone who is both an able networker and an effective facilitator of relationships. She is probably interpersonally adroit and astute with people. She is likely to make leaps of thought in a conversation as her mind creates links between pieces of information. She will want to know all about the process of the coaching programme you are proposing: what it involves, the kind of material you want to cover and how you will do that. She will also enjoy an evolutionary coaching process and so will want to know how much room you will build in for changes of direction and spontaneity. Her natural style will be to leave things open-ended with room for manoeuvre, so it is best not to press her for a decision about whether or not to work with you before she is ready to give it. Focus the sales conversation on what you can do for her and highlight the ways in which working with you will give her more tools for getting things done. This potential client wants to enjoy relationships and would like to be seen as entertaining. She'd like to think that working with you will be stimulating for you and that you will enjoy her company as well. She is looking for an inspiring coach, someone who will get her to look at her situation in new ways and who will extend her natural people-handling capabilities. This potential client will be swayed by whether or not she thinks that you will be a coach who is able to simultaneously accept her and challenge her in relation to her coaching goals.*

In reality, most clients are likely to use a combination of two or three of these styles simultaneously.

If you have considered the four cameos in relation to a recent sales conversation – or if you are not yet selling, a recent conversation with a business contact – you might now like to answer the following questions about that conversation. Jot down your answers in the space below each question if you wish, or use a separate notebook.

What style, or combination of styles, did the person you were speaking with use?

What did you observe about the person that led you to this conclusion?

In what ways did the information you included in your conversation meet their style needs?

In what ways did the information you included in your sales conversation not meet their style needs?

Given your conclusions about the style, or styles, that the person used, what would you do differently if you could start that conversation over again?

At the end of the day, the more practice you have the more effective a sales person you'll become. You will find your own way and learn as you go along. Perhaps the most important thing you can do for yourself as you learn to sell is to ask yourself after each sales conversation: 'What could I have done differently and better to have had greater influence with that person?'

Your marketing materials

The next portion of this chapter is going to focus on your marketing materials. We have already discussed one form of marketing material – the coaching programme outline. This is the document you produce for a client after they have become interested in working with you that describes the process of the work you could do together. We are now going to examine other written marketing materials which you might need earlier on in the sales process. These marketing materials are there to help you create client interest in the first place, interest which will hopefully result in you earning the right to produce a written programme outline for a particular client.

Your first decision must be whether or not you want to produce these materials yourself or whether you want to employ professional firms to do so for you. This is very much your choice and there are pros and cons to both ways of doing it. If you keep the writing and production of your marketing materials in-house you will need to consider the following factors:

- ☐ your costs will not go up;

- ☐ you will retain control of the materials;

- ☐ you can make improvements to them and update them whenever you want;

- ☐ you will be thoroughly familiar with your own marketing material and hence will find it easier to recall them in your conversations with clients;

- ☐ you will need to be an effective writer and, for your website, you must understand html code;

- ☐ you will have to be prepared to sit down and regularly review the content of your materials;

- ☐ you will probably need access to graphics and artwork software for your written materials, and webpage editing software for your website;

- ☐ you will have the ongoing opportunity to improve your marketing skills as you continually update your materials.

Alternatively, if you decide to hire professional firms to write and produce your marketing materials for you will need to consider these issues:

☐ your costs will go up;

☐ you will need to invest time in explaining to the firms what you do, how you do it and how you want to describe your coaching offer to clients;

☐ you will need to pay them periodically to update your materials as your coaching offer and website evolve;

☐ you may find that the words and phrases they use to describe your coaching offer are not ones that trip easily off your tongue as you talk to clients and that there is a subsequent disconnection between you and your materials in the minds of some of your clients;

☐ you will have professionally produced, visually impressive marketing materials that will present your coaching business effectively and compellingly.

Whichever decision you make you will need to give some thought to what you want to include in each of your marketing materials. You will have to bring your coaching programmes to life as you describe them to your clients, but your materials will still play a very important part in keeping you and your offer in the minds of your clients.

The next few sections of this chapter will examine a variety of marketing materials, exploring whether or not you need them. If you do, we shall be talking a look at what you could include in:

☐ your logo;

☐ your brochure;

☐ your website;

☐ your advertisements;

☐ your business cards, letter-headed paper and compliments slips;

☐ your other promotional materials.

Your logo

The purpose of a logo is to provide your clients and potential clients with a symbol of both yourself and your business: a visual image that is readily identifiable with your coaching offer which will stick in their minds. When a client sees your logo on a business card or letter-headed paper, a website or any other marketing material you will want them to recognize it immediately and automatically think of you.

You don't have to have a logo but it's a good idea to do so. If you decide to have one you will need to find a symbol that you like, one that is presented in colours you are keen on and one that means something to you. You don't have to spend money on having one designed for you, although you could do so if you wanted to, or you could design one yourself. If you do decide to have a logo you will need to include it on every piece of marketing material that you produce to maximize its effect and to make sure that everything you send to a client or potential is branded in the same way.

Your brochure

The purpose of your brochure is to provide your clients and potential clients with some general written information about who you are, what you do and what's in it for them should they decide to work with you. A client who likes to think, reflect and read before coming to a decision will find your brochure a valuable reference point after a sales conversation with you. You can also send it out in advance of going to meet a client. Remember, the key point is to put information into your brochure which, from a client's point of view, is both relevant and informative. It doesn't have to include every detail about you. It does, however, need to present a convincing case that you have something worthwhile to offer potential clients.

If you decide to produce a brochure you might like to include the following information in it.

- ☐ A succinct description of your coaching offer – what you do, the issues you work with clients on and the outcomes that clients can expect from working with you.

- ☐ A summary of your background experience and qualifications as a coach.

- ☐ Examples of objectives from any of your recent coaching programmes. Suitable examples, depending on your coaching specialism, could be:
  - assisting a sole-practitioner in a busy printing business to balance her life and work commitments effectively;
  - helping a hardworking but ineffective manager to develop the influencing skills and interpersonal impact he needs to work effectively with his peer group.

- ☐ If you don't yet have any recent coaching examples, and want to identify areas in which you rate yourself as a coach, suitable one-liners, depending on your coaching specialism, could be:
  - helping clients handle and respond to conflict in their lives more effectively;

57

    — assisting technically minded managers to develop the selling and influencing skills they need to work effectively with a range of customers.

It is also vital that you include in your brochure:

☐ your contact details for your telephone(s), email and website;

☐ your evolving client list.

Your client list can prove particularly useful as it will demonstrate your range of experience and provide credible evidence for your claim that you are an effective coach. If you don't yet have any clients, make sure that you provide details of your background experience instead and explain the ways in which your previous life, work and qualifications have prepared you to be employed as an effective coach. This section will enable your existing clients and any potential clients to read about your background and come to their own conclusions about your credibility.

Having your brochure available as an email attachment as well as on paper will provide you with the flexibility to work in whichever way suits your clients. There is no right or wrong length to a brochure, nor is there a right or wrong page size either. Your brochure needs to be long enough to include what you need to say, and it can be in A5 or A4 or any page size you choose. However, do make sure that you like its format and presentation so that, when you come to give it to a client or potential client, you can do so with confidence.

Your website

Much of the world works online and you need to do so as well. However elaborate or simple your website is, it needs to:

☐ describe what you do;

☐ provide a taster of your services;

☐ be visually attractive and professionally presented;

☐ give your contact details;

☐ detail your evolving client list.

Having a reasonably short website that you can update and change as your business grows is a viable option. Software exists that can enable you, working from the desk in your office, to change the wording on your webpage and upload it to the World Wide Web. This way of working will allow you to make small but important changes to your website (like adding names to your client list) as and when you need to, without having to hire a website design company and then wait for them to make the changes for you. Your software supplier will be able to take you through the options for purchasing this kind of software, which represents excellent value for the flexibility it will provide you with.

Advertisements

You need to make a decision about whether or not you want to advertise your business. Some coaches choose not do so. They rely instead on referral and repeat business and make this a virtue by telling potential clients that they don't advertise. Imparting this piece of information to a potential client emphasizes that these coaches don't need to advertise and that their existing clients advertise for them through word of mouth. It is highly worthwhile for you to be able to tell this to any potential clients as it clearly demonstrates how much your existing clients rate your coaching service.

However, other equally effective and successful coaches do advertise and in the end the choice is yours. If you want to use advertisements to promote your business you will need to consider where you want to advertise. You will have to find places that will promote your business to people who are specifically interested in coaching and in your coaching specialism, and this must be within the locality where you want to develop your business. Trade magazines or coaching journals would be good places to start.

Your business cards, letter-headed paper and compliments slips

Depending on how you decide to promote your business you may or may not need letter-headed paper and compliments slips. Many coaches contact their clients by telephone and email, and invoice them via email as well. As a result they don't require letter-headed paper. Others still use some letter-headed paper for invoicing and perhaps compliments slips for certain times as well. The choice is yours depending on your preferences for how you contact your clients, send them written materials and bill them.

However, almost every coach needs a business card. Business cards are very useful to clients as they act as a quick reference point for your name, contact details and what you do. If you are going to invest in business cards you will need to think carefully about what to include on these in addition to the obvious information about your name and how to get hold of you. For instance, do you want to:

☐ describe yourself as a coach, or as a coach working in one of the niches e.g. a life coach or as an executive coach?

☐ include your coaching qualifications and your non-coaching qualifications, or simply your coaching qualifications?

☐ include any other information, such as a single-line description of the benefit to clients of working with you?

Basically, you need to look at all this from a client's perspective. From their viewpoint, if including any or all of these kinds of information will make what you do more, rather than less clear, then it is worth your while to include them. But if adding any of these three things will only muddy the water, it is better to omit them. Remember, your business card is both a form of marketing as well as a reminder of how to get in contact with you. As with any other form of marketing it must not confuse clients about who you are and what you do. There are a great many coaches out there. Your job is to make it transparently clear to clients and potential clients what it is you do, how you do it and how they can get hold of you. Keep it simple and clear-cut on your business cards.

One last thing: if you do decide to use any of the above forms of marketing and you do have a logo, remember to include it on all of them.

Other promotional materials

Here I would include paper pads, pens and writing equipment; other stationery or office equipment; banner stands; and just about any item that can be liveried in your logo, if you have one, and with your name, contact details and what you do printed on it. The purpose of these promotional materials is to keep your name in the minds of your clients. You don't have to use any of them, but if you do, try to make sure that the information on them is clear, succinct and makes sense from a client's perspective. Remember, the way you behave with your clients and potential clients is your most influential selling tool, so the purpose of all these other promotional materials, such as the items listed above, is simply to act as a reminder to clients of who you are, what you do and how they can contact you.

Having taken a look at the main marketing materials you could use in the preceding sections, it might be worth your while taking a few minutes to jot down your thoughts about them. If you want to you can to use the space below to make a note about the specific marketing materials you will want to employ, along with any other important issues that come to your mind which may relate to them. Alternatively you may prefer to use a separate notebook.

In what follows I am going to focus on a series of sales and marketing-related issues:

☐ asking for a client reference;

☐ asking for referral business;

☐ developing a mission statement;

☐ working as an associate;

☐ and how much to charge.

Asking for a client reference

This is an important issue. Having an existing client, or preferably several, willing to speak with a potential client about the quality of your work can make all the difference to those people who are unable to decide whether or not to work with you. You will find that some potential clients will prefer to make up their minds by themselves, in conversation with you, about whether or not to work with you. Others will prefer to speak with someone who has benefitted from your services so they can ask about their experiences of working with you.

If you find that a sales process is stalling, you might want to offer a potential client the option of speaking with someone who has worked with you in the past as a way of getting the dialogue going again. This option will give that potential client a welcome opportunity to discuss the issues that are causing them to stall with someone other than you. As your business evolves, you will need to make sure that any clients you decide to approach for a reference have worked with you in the not too distant past. Suggesting that a stalled potential client speaks with someone who last worked with you six months or a year ago might make them wonder why they are being asked to seek out someone you worked with a while ago, and whether this means that your more recent coaching programmes haven't gone too well.

In asking a client to provide a reference for you, it is best to avoid doing so in a way that puts that client on the spot. You could, therefore, wait until you need a reference and then email your selected client(s) with your request. Or alternatively you could pose a hypothetical question to a client, again via email, on completion of a coaching programme. This could then establish whether or not they'd be willing to provide you with a reference in the future, should the need arise, by speaking with another potential client.

If you don't yet have any clients to call on in this way, and are thinking that it would be useful to provide a potential client with a reference point, it might be worthwhile asking someone from your coaching course to provide you with a reference. A course tutor, or the course director, provided they know you well enough to provide an informed opinion, would be good places to start.

Asking for referral business

Potentially, this is a great way to grow your business whereby those who've enjoyed and benefitted from working with you will tell their contacts about you or will provide you with their contacts' details so you can get in touch with them. However, do remember that asking for referral business is also a potentially awkward position to put a client in, and many people will baulk at being asked to 'tap up' their family, friends and business contacts in this way. You will need to judge this one carefully.

What is significant here is your decision about who to approach in this way, and how you will word your questions when you make your approach. Initially, it may be appropriate to ask if they know of anyone else who might be interested in talking with you. If you pose this as a closed question which begs a yes/no answer, it will then be easy for your client to say 'no' and move straight on if they need to. If they answer 'yes', you could then ask a supplementary question about how they would recommend you get in touch with this contact. This kind of open question will enable your client to specify either that they will make the introduction when they judge the time is right, or that they will ask their contact to see if they want to take things forward and then get back to you; or that they'll provide you with the contact details you need themselves. You will need to decide whether to ask these questions face to face or via email. Either option could work for you, depending on the circumstances and the quality of your working relationship with them.

Your mission statement

The key issues here are whether or not you need a mission statement, and if you decide it would be useful to have one, what role you want the mission statement to play in the selling and marketing of your business. Many coaches do not have a mission statement, and run very effective coaching practices without one. To help you decide if you want to invest in developing a mission statement or not, let's start with the role it could play in your selling and marketing activity.

A mission statement consists of a paragraph describing what you and your business can do and usually the values you will incorporate to accomplish these things. If you believe that having such a statement will add value to your business – by clarifying for your clients what you do and how you do it – then it might be worth investing your time in developing one. In this case you may want to consider how you will use your mission statement. Is it something that you will:

- use in the sales process when speaking with clients?

- incorporate into your brochure?

- include in your coaching programme outlines?

- leave with those clients you have met face to face with as a reminder of what you can do for them?

- display in your office as an aide-memoire of key points when selling to clients on the telephone?

However, if you are already clear – or are about to be, with a bit more concerted thought – on how you are going to tell clients what you can achieve as a coach, you might be thinking at this point that all the time and effort you would have to put into producing a mission statement would be better applied to your other selling and marketing activities.

Working as an associate coach

This can be a very good way of getting experience and confidence as a new coach. You will still be running your own business and working as your own boss, but at least part of the work you undertake will be on behalf of a different coaching business for whom you work on a contract basis. Many coaching consultancies, and some more broadly based consultancies, work with associate coaches. This way of working suits them because they:

☐ don't incur employer's National Insurance contributions through working with associates;

☐ do benefit from having a wider range of coaches to call on than those they employ directly.

It is worth noting that this arrangement might suit you as well because you would be:

☐ earning income;

☐ getting experience;

☐ learning from working with a pool of coaches;

☐ finding your feet as a commercially focused coach.

If you like this idea you might want to contact suitable consultancies in the geographical area where you want to develop business and put the suggestion to them.

How much to charge

Basically, you will have to charge what your coaching services are worth, and here you must decide for yourself what that should be. The following matters go hand in hand:

☐ Knowing that your proposed coaching programme will help a particular client achieve their coaching goals.

☐ Believing that as a result it represents excellent value to that client.

☐ Talking with your client about what it will cost them to work with you on the coaching programme.

☐ Doing so with confidence and ease.

It is quite straightforward to tell a client what you charge if you believe that your coaching programme will meet their needs, you have already demonstrated this to them and gained their respect, they are committed to reading a coaching programme outline you're going to write for them and they are already excited about the possibility of working with you. The danger for coaches talking about their charges comes from not having done a good enough job earlier on in convincing a client they can help them, and then starting to speak too soon about the cost of a programme. This can come across to clients as premature and clumsy.

Charging too much or too little

However, there are also pitfalls for coaches who get it wrong by either over-charging or under-charging. If you charge too little, you will undermine yourself and drop the thought into your potential clients' minds that you might not be rating your services as highly as you could do. Equally, if you charge too much you will price yourself out of work as clients will quickly cotton on to the idea that they can get a comparable or better service for less money elsewhere. The best way to grow your business and earn a good living from it year on year is to provide a valued service to clients at a price that is fair. In this scenario your clients will stand by you, refer you, tell their contacts about you and come back for more. How you behave with them is vital to this, but so is what you charge.

Purchasers of coaching services are becoming more and more sophisticated at making informed choices about the coaches they work with, and are also likely to be up to date about what the appropriate price range should be for a particular coach. Doing your own homework on what other coaches in your niche and geographical location are charging will stand you in good stead when deciding what you want to charge. Talking to your coaching qualification course director about suitable fees would be a good place to start.

Structuring your fees

Your fee structure must make sense to your clients. It needs to be simple, transparent and clear, both in terms of what you charge and when you will apply a charge to an invoice. One of your starting points could be to decide whether you want to charge:

☐ an hourly rate;

☐ a daily or half day rate;

☐ a price for a complete programme.

These decisions will depend on how long your coaching meetings typically are, whether your coaching work is largely bespoke or largely pre-structured, and whether or not you want to charge the same fee for delivering a coaching meeting as for, say, undertaking research. Personally, I think a coach's fee rate should not alter with the kind of activity they are undertaking on behalf of their client, although a few coaches do vary their fees in this way. It makes more sense to charge the same fee structure for any coaching programme-related activity, such as undertaking research or questionnaire analysis, or designing coaching processes and delivering coaching meetings. To do otherwise could be misconstrued as the coach giving equal importance to a range of activities.

Having decided what your fee structure will be, you will need to become practised and relaxed at telling your clients about it and about how much you charge. If you are comfortable with your fees, most of your clients will be too. When coaches start to swallow hard before saying how much they charge, or tell potential clients that they hate talking about money, they can start to undercut their own effectiveness. Indeed, you may well *feel* somewhat nervous about speaking about your charges, especially early on in your selling activity, and you may *hate* talking about money with clients – but don't say either of these things to any client who is thinking of working with you. You don't need to. Focus instead on the extent to which your coaching programme will help that client reach their coaching goals and tell them how much you'd like to charge them to help them get there. Focus as well on the positive outcomes and the facts of the situation: that you can help them, that you will do so and that you want to start as soon as possible. Then you must let the client decide for themselves whether or not they want to work with you at the price you wish to charge.

SUMMARY

We have spent some considerable time examining your selling and marketing activity, materials and related issues because as a sole practitioner your skill in handling these aspects of your business is crucial. It is as critical to the eventual success of your coaching practice as your skills as a coach. As with learning any new set of skills you might initially find all of this hard going, and may have to apply yourself dedicatedly to the task of learning to sell and market your business. Or you may take to it straightaway. Either way, don't give up – when you do have a set-back, pick yourself up, step back from the situation, evaluate what you could have done differently and what you can do better next time round, and begin again.

We now need to focus our attention on how you can construct and maintain a working relationship with each one of your clients.

5

YOUR RELATIONSHIPS WITH YOUR CLIENTS

One of the things that initially surprised me in my work as a coach was how often I was the only person in a client's working life who was actively listening to them. For many of my executive coaching clients, most of their other working relationships are characterized either by them listening to other people – their clients, their team members, their senior managers, their peers, the regulators – or by them seeking to meet other people's expectations of them – their own, their clients', their senior managers', their peers', the regulators'. I was unprepared for how infrequently anyone listened to them in the course of an average day.

You may also prove to be the only person in the lives of some of your clients who is prepared to listen and understand their point of view. You could be the only person who sets out to appreciate their perspective on the circumstances they want to speak with you about. It is a truism to say that a coach's role involves active listening. It is also a truism to say that most clients will want to speak about themselves during a coaching meeting and will expect to be heard. Indeed, some clients would believe that first and foremost they are paying a coach to listen to them and gain some understanding of them before they even think about offering any coaching input at all. In addition, clients will expect additional things from you as their coach depending on their various learning and listening styles and their coaching goals.

This chapter will help you get to grips with what these additional things might be. It will outline what expectations your clients may have of you, assist you in thinking through the dynamics of your relationships with your clients and help you make some decisions about how to present your coaching qualification to them.

What clients will expect from their coach

Different clients will have different expectations of their coach. It is a good idea to explore what these expectations might be early on in a coaching relationship so that, firstly, you will be aware of the criteria against which your client will be judging your performance and, secondly, you will have the opportunity to readjust their expectations if they are unrealistic. Client expectations are likely to include the following:

STRUCTURE

Most clients will expect their coach to provide them with a written process that is appropriate to their coaching needs, and they will want to see a copy of this programme outline before the start of the first meeting. They will also expect their coach to actively manage the ongoing coaching process to ensure that it is as useful as possible to them as the client once they get started. This might mean that for a few of your clients the process will need to be amended part-way through, to take a particular set of emerging circumstances into account. For most clients, however, such detours will be minimal if the programme has been made suitable for their requirements right from the start.

DIRECTION

Most clients will be content to allow you as their coach to set the direction for the coaching programme and will be willing to follow your lead. One of the real pleasures in participating as a client in a coaching programme is to let someone who is qualified, inter-personally able and there to assist you manage a process from which you can learn, grow and develop.

INPUT

Clients come to coaching to learn something new. Their expectation will be that this process will provide them with new angles, new points of view, new perspectives and new ideas by which they can make decisions and/or achieve sustained behaviour change. They will also expect that you will provide input to the process to enable them to realize their coaching goals and that you will therefore play an active part in helping them to make the changes they need to make.

How you do this is a matter for you as an individual. Some coaches will make extensive use of data on their clients which they have collected from questionnaires. They then use such data to provide their clients with insight and development. Other coaches will prefer to listen to their clients talking about specific significant events in their lives before they facilitate a conversation about those experiences, the aim here being that the client will come to their own conclusions about what they need to do differently and better. Alternatively, some coaches will choose to collect qualitative data from people who work with or know their client, such as their colleagues and customers, depending on the objectives of the coaching programme.

My preference is to use business psychology to help clients learn about their intra-personal world, and then to ask my clients to work with professional actors in tailor-made role-plays and scenarios to learn new behaviours that are directly related to their coaching goals. Whatever methods and processes you use, the important aspect here is to provide your client with what they are looking for – new, enlightening input and feedback that will help them attain their coaching goals and achieve sustained behaviour change.

RELATIONSHIP

The quality of the relationship which you build with your client is central to the effectiveness of the coaching programme. Your role as coach can be, variously, to act as a sounding board, facilitator, supportive challenger and effective questioner of your client. In all of these roles your goal must be to provide your client with an opportunity to learn, to see themselves and their coaching issues from another, more fruitful perspective, and to assist them in moving closer to attaining their coaching goals. I think it is very difficult to play any of these roles as a coach if you do not set out at the start of a coaching meeting, as a conscious choice, to concern yourself fully with:

- ☐ what your client is saying to you at the time they are saying it;

- ☐ what they need from the current coaching meeting to help them take the next step;

- ☐ how they are responding both to you and to what you are saying;

- ☐ how effective the current coaching meeting is in assisting them to move towards their coaching goals.

At the end of the day, the extent to which you as the coach can meet the expectations of each of your clients is the extent to which your business will grow by referral, repeat business, word of mouth and reputation.

Establishing trust

This needs to happen early on if your client is to make effective use of the time they spend with you. In my view, the onus is on you as the coach to create the circumstances in which your client chooses to trust you. Working to a strict confidentiality agreement is essential, as is working to strict ethical guidelines. Being able to tell your client that you work with a supervisor is also important. Being clear in your mind as to how and why your proposed coaching process will meet the needs of your client, and clearly communicating this information to your client, will help too as will any time spent helping each client to understand how and why the process you propose will enable them to reach their coaching goals. All these things take time, and the investment you make upfront in talking through these issues with your client will pay rich dividends in the subsequent coaching work you do together. Clients will come to realize that you have invested this time with them at the start of the programme because you want the process to be as effective as possible, and they will see you are prepared to work hard to make sure that it hits the spot.

Why clients will choose one coach over another

Choosing which coach to work with is very personal for each client. Some clients will choose a coach to work with because that coach is very different to them in style and approach. These clients will want to work with someone who is likely to challenge them in those areas that they see as weaknesses for them, or even as blind spots. Other clients will choose to work with a coach because that person is someone they like, who they think they'll get on well with and will enjoy working with. Whatever choice they make, your clients will need to feel comfortable enough with you that they will be able to speak openly about the issues they face. They will also need to have faith in your skill and judgement to deal effectively with these issues.

While there is very little you can do once a client has made up their mind to work with someone else, there is plenty you can do beforehand to ensure that they make an informed choice about you and your work. You need to have enough self-awareness to be able to give a potential client an accurate picture of who you are, how you coach and what you can offer them. Helping a client to make the right choice for them will mean that some may decide not to work with you. This is preferable if the alternative is that they elect to work with you under a misapprehension about who you are, how you work or what working with you will mean to them. In this case, a client may become very annoyed indeed at some point in the coaching process if they come to the conclusion that you as their coach are not proving to be the person they were expecting to work with. If you are transparently clear and upfront about how you work and who you are this should pre-empt such an unfortunate situation and this will mean that those clients who do opt to work with you have done so because you are the right coach for them.

What your coaching qualification means to you and your clients

There are many, many coaching qualifications out there, and they come in all shapes and sizes. There are some courses that involve a process of a few weeks to train a coach in a life coaching model and related material. There are MSc-level qualifications which take up to a year or more that will result in a coach gaining a professionally recognized coaching qualification. There are coach accreditation courses that are recognized by professional coaching bodies such as the Association for Coaching. And there are numerous other qualifications and accreditation processes in between. So assuming that you are part-accredited as a coach or have already qualified as a coach, let me ask you: what do you think your coaching qualification means to your clients and potential clients? If you wish to, use the space below to jot down your answer, or use a separate notebook.

Now let me ask you another question: what does your coaching qualification mean to you? Again, the space below can be used or a separate notebook to jot down your answers.

Let's think about what you've written. Many organizations currently employ coaches to work with their managers and staff. Many individual people also choose to employ coaches to work with them directly. Thankfully, both organizations and members of the public are becoming more sophisticated at understanding the difference between effective and ineffective coaching services, and as such they are requiring increasing levels of professionalism from the coaches they employ. Typically, to be deemed effective, coaches need to have an accredited coaching qualification and must work within strict ethical and confidentiality boundaries together with a supervisor.

You might like to take a look back at what you have written. To what extent does it reflect these imperatives? Working one to one with any client is likely to mean that that client is, to some extent, vulnerable and open. As a coach, you need to use the influence you have wisely and be mindful that what you say to any client you are working with can have a significant impact on the way they:

☐ view themselves;

☐ see other people;

☐ look at their life and relationships;

☐ frame what they believe.

The responsibility to work well with any client is yours, and in seeking to work as a coach you must be mindful of the possibility that exists for you to exceed the boundaries of your competence and stray into areas for which you are not equipped. Working to strict ethical standards, with a supervisor and in total confidentiality, are minimum requirements that you need to follow to work wisely and safely with your clients. So what does your coaching qualification mean? It ought to mean that you are:

☐ clear about the parameters of your competence;

☐ able to coach effectively within those parameters;

☐ willing to draw the line for any client between what you can work with them on and what you cannot work with them on.

At this point let's revisit the two questions I posed earlier. I'd like to ask them again here in a slightly different form. What do you want your coaching qualification to mean to your clients? You might like to use the space below to jot down your answer, or use a separate notebook.

And what do you want your coaching qualification to mean to you? Once again, you might like to use the space below to jot down your answer or use a separate notebook.

You'll recall that in Chapter 2 you considered how to describe your coaching offer to your clients. Looking back at what you wrote then, is there anything you'd now like to add to the description you generated, given that you have reviewed what your coaching qualification means? Should you wish to, use the space below to include anything you'd like to add to your description of your coaching offer, or use a separate notebook.

The boundary between you and your clients

One of the key boundaries you need to establish and maintain is that between you and your clients. The role of coach is a very specific one that enables you, in the normal course of your work, to get to know your clients well and much more quickly than would be the case in everyday life. In the course of your work you will learn a lot about your clients in a short space of time. You are likely find out about their areas of strength as people as well as what they enjoy doing, what they like and don't like, what they find stressful and challenging in their lives, what they struggle with and what they don't have much aptitude for. In short, you will find out a good deal about them and you'll get to know them well. In the course of an effective coaching relationship you will come to know who your client is.

The temptation for some coaches, when they like and enjoy working with a particular client, is to move that relationship into a social context. This is also a temptation for clients as well, especially if they are not used to having much support in their lives and are enjoying this contact with their coach. Here I would ask you to consider the following scenario: a client suggests having a beer with you after your coaching meeting. You, as their coach, don't want to appear rude or jeopardize the rapport and trust you have developed with your client and so you go along for that one beer. Once you accept such an invitation to go to the bar or the pub and have a drink, your relationship with that client will have changed. You will no longer be a professional advisor to that client. You have become someone who also socializes with them.

For some of you, with some of your clients, this may not present a problem to your working effectively together thereafter. But for others it might. Why? Because the professional boundaries that you need to set up and maintain to keep a coaching relationship viable have to preclude anything but professional coach/client contact during the lifetime of the coaching programme. You have to maintain your professional distance in order to be as objective and as effective as possible. This doesn't mean you can't be warm and engaging. But it does mean that you need to remain sufficiently emotionally separate from your client to be able to challenge him or her effectively, question him or her insightfully, act as a productive sounding board and be a supportive facilitator of the coaching process. Your ability to adequately perform these functions could be compromised if you socialize with your clients.

SUMMARY

This chapter has discussed what your clients might expect from you, how you can meet their expectations, what your qualification means to you and some of the boundary issues between you and your clients. Let's now go on to consider supervision.

6

WORKING WITH A SUPERVISOR

As a professional coach you need to work, on a regular and ongoing basis, with an experienced, effective supervisor. You need to do this to ensure the quality of your work as far as your clients are concerned and for your own development. Simply put, it's good practice to work with a supervisor and unwise, to say the least, not to. Many of you may be new to supervision or may not have had experience of effective supervision. You may not see the point of it, or you may see it as an expensive luxury and be tempted to start to work as a coach without the services of a supervisor. After all, working with a supervisor will increase your costs just when you are starting up your business. However, you simply cannot afford to take this risk, either for yourself or for your clients. Both you and your clients will benefit from sustained and professional supervision, and you need to make a purposeful commitment to work with a supervisor from the off.

A supervisor's role is to act as an experienced, objective sounding board for you, to be someone who is outside your coaching relationships but able to provide input. As many of the dynamics in a coach's relationship with their supervisor mimic the very difficulties they are having in their coaching relationships, working with an effective supervisor can be a vital source of development and learning for even the most experienced of coaches.

Supervision has its roots in social work, therapy and clinical psychology where it has been standard practice for a long time. However, supervision is still relatively new in the coaching profession and is largely a matter of individual conscience. This chapter will examine the role of a supervisor and outline the benefits of working with a supervisor to your practice and clients. It will also suggest some of the key risks you face if you don't work with a supervisor, and provide you with some pointers to help you select a supervisor who will add value to your work as a coach.

The role of a supervisor

Different coaches need different things from their supervisors. As someone new to coaching you are likely to expect and want different input from your supervisor compared to an executive coach who has been working with clients for years. So what can you, as a newly qualified coach, expect from a supervisor?

WORKING WITH A SUPERVISOR

An effective supervisor will be able to provide you with:

☐ an opportunity to reflect on the progress and direction of your coaching programmes, ensuring that you are offering the best coaching you can to your clients;

☐ practical support in the form of ideas, suggestions, feedback and new perspectives on the coaching work you are doing with your clients;

☐ relational support as a supportive sounding board to whom you can pose questions about your coaching work, your clients, your reactions to your clients and any concerns you may have about a particular coaching programme or meeting;

☐ ongoing professional development in the form of learning about yourself as a coach – your strengths and areas for development – as well as how to improve your core coaching skills and enhance your knowledge base as a coach.

Even though working with a supervisor will inevitably put your business costs up – depending on how often you want to meet with them and how much they charge you – it will still be well worth your financial investment for the peace of mind, development and performance improvements that effective supervision will create for you, your business and your clients. Hopefully, working with an effective supervisor will result, over time, in you regarding them as an invaluable source of wisdom, experience, insight and knowledge.

So, if you are going to work with a supervisor, what benefits can you expect to accrue from the work? The benefits of supervision to you, the coach, include:

☐ accepting or sharing responsibility for ensuring the quality of your work in relation to the coaching programmes and client issues that you decide to discuss;

☐ listening to you describe your coaching work, before picking up on and confronting issues you need to learn from or see in a different light;

☐ acting as a sounding board and consultant for you to discuss any concerns you may have about a particular coaching programme or client;

☐ offering you feedback and providing you with direction that will result in performance improvements in your coaching skills, theoretical knowledge base and personal coaching attributes.

The process of a supervision meeting

Your supervision meetings will likely be about an hour long and be scheduled at regular intervals, depending on how much coaching work you are doing at any one time. They could take the form of one-to-one meetings between you and your supervisor, or you might elect for group peer supervision where a number of coaches meet together and their supervisor leads the meeting. You may prefer the group environment first of all but in actual fact, you'll get better value overall from dedicated one-to-one supervision time.

During a supervision meeting you will describe either a specific coaching programme or a set of coaching issues that you'd like to discuss with your supervisor. The subsequent input from your supervisor should enable you to step back from the actual work itself and:

□ reflect on what you are doing, how you are doing it and the extent to which you need to adjust your approach to offer best value to your client or clients;

□ acquire a fuller understanding of what you need to learn to do differently and better, if anything, so that you can provide the best coaching you can offer to your clients;

□ receive guidance, reassurance and support aimed at improving your work as a coach with a specific client or set of client issues.

The risks of working without a supervisor

As well as missing out on all the growth, development and performance improvements that effective supervision will bring to you, working without a supervisor carries a risk. Basically, you could mess up and fail to learn from the experience, or you could mess up and fail to notice that you'd made a mistake in the first place. In either case, you might continue to work in less than optimal ways with successive clients and ultimately could do wrong by your clients and to your business. Of course, working with a supervisor will not guarantee that you do not err. But it will mean that you have an experienced eye overseeing the work you choose to discuss with your supervisor, and it will mean that you have someone objective to go to should you need to talk anything through.

Unfortunately, some coaches do still work without a supervisor. Often, those coaches who are tempted to work in this way do so because they believe they don't need supervision. They think they already have the experience, knowledge and skills they need to coach effectively with any and all clients. Sadly, these are often the very people who don't reflect enough on their own practice and develop blind spots over time. Other coaches do recognize the need to talk client issues through with an objective colleague but, instead of finding and paying for professional supervision, they prefer to speak informally with a peer as and when they meet up. The choice is, of course, yours but, bearing in mind that some of the professional coaching bodies require their members to be in ongoing professional supervision, it is increasingly difficult to justify practising as a coach and not investing in a relationship with a supervisor (see the Useful Weblinks section at the end of the book).

What do you want out of working with a supervisor?

Some coaches select a supervisor who works in their niche but has a lot more experience. Others choose to work with a supervisor who has a different, but related, background because they value the different perspective that their supervisor will bring to their discussions. Either option could prove effective for you provided that you are able to speak openly with your supervisor. There is no point choosing a highly recommended and well qualified supervisor and finding that you can't talk to them. You need to be able to tell your supervisor honestly what you want to tell them, and feel that they will be able to deal in a straightforward and clear manner with the issues you put to them. Of course, you and your supervisor might not hit it off straightaway and you might need to work at developing a candid and open relationship with one another. But if, despite all your efforts, you still don't find their input or their way of responding to you helpful, sack the supervisor and find another one. Don't give up on supervision.

In order to help you think through what might be involved for you in working with a supervisor, and to help you decide what input you'd like from a supervisor, you might like to consider the following questions. If you wish to, you can use the space below each one to jot down your answer or, alternatively, you may prefer to use a separate notebook.

What qualities and skills are you looking for in a supervisor?

What professional background or experience would you like your supervisor to have?

What, if any, are your concerns about working with a supervisor?

For what specific purposes do you want to meet with a supervisor?

‘ *How often do you want to meet with a supervisor?* ’

‘ *What else is important for you to clarify with a supervisor before you start to work with them?* ’

SUMMARY

We have examined the case for having supervision and explored the role that effective supervision can play in your coaching business and in your ongoing professional development. Let's now examine in detail how you are going to manage that ongoing professional development, in all its varied forms, in the next chapter.

7

YOUR ONGOING PROFESSIONAL DEVELOPMENT

Your business is going well. You are working as a coach with existing clients and are developing new business relationships with potential clients. You are enjoying running your own business and take pleasure in being your own boss. However, you recognize that, even though things are going well for you, you cannot rest there. You need to continually upgrade your skills, knowledge and competencies as a coach if you are to have something fresh and original to offer to your clients. To focus your own development programme effectively, you could do with some feedback. You'd like to know how you are doing as a coach as opposed to a salesperson or the owner of a business. You'd like to know more about your coaching strengths and weaknesses and in what areas you could improve your performance.

This chapter will focus on your ongoing professional development. It will take you through the options for evaluating your own performance as a coach, help you determine which ones are most feasible for you and help you decide how to manage your own continuous learning and development. Let's first look at some of the key issues before going on to examine your options for handling them.

Developing yourself as a coach

Some of you reading this may be thinking that the lack of detailed feedback on the quality of your performance as a coach is an issue that doesn't matter too much. You may be satisfied with the knowledge that your clients, their managers and their learning and development or human resources partners approve of the work you are doing for them. You may be comfortable knowing that, as long as clients want to work with you, your performance must be pretty satisfactory. Others of you may be thinking that the lack of ongoing feedback on your performance is something you would like to address, especially those of you used to regular appraisals as part of your previous employed life. As a sole practitioner you no longer have these benchmarks against which to evaluate your performance. Instead, you must decide for yourself how well you are doing, set your own criteria against which to measure your performance, and determine for yourselves in what areas you need to develop further skills and competencies.

The fact is you simply must plan for and devote time and effort to developing your core coaching skills, tools, competencies and abilities. You cannot do otherwise. You need to learn and develop so that you have something new to offer your clients. Even though every client is an individual person with a unique history and a unique set of requirements from their coaching programme, and could therefore relate to the same coaching meeting in very different ways, you cannot simply repeat for one what you've done for another year after year after year and expect your coaching programmes to be effective for each person. You will get bored and fall behind the competition. Your competitors will be updating their offers, they will be keeping abreast of new research, and they will be keeping up to date with changes and developments in their clients' workplaces. If you are not doing the same, your clients will not get the best value from you. Your business will suffer.

You must build on your coaching qualification and add regularly to your coaching skills, tools, competencies and abilities. You must plan for your own development and find ways of achieving your development goals. The key point is that you need to make it a regular part of your business planning and include a budget for your own development.

Eliciting feedback from clients

Even for coaches whose businesses are thriving, the question of what feedback to elicit from clients, and when to elicit it, can be a taxing one. Indirectly, a thriving coaching business is a good indicator that you are doing a lot of things effectively as a coach. You can infer from the numbers of clients who want to work with you that they rate you highly enough to choose to work with you. You can deduce from the amount of referral business you are getting that your clients tell other people about how effective a coach you are. These are useful indicators but they are not going to give you the detailed feedback on your coaching skills and competencies that you want or help you identify in what areas you need to develop.

ASKING CLIENTS FOR FEEDBACK

You can, of course, ask your clients for feedback. You could do this when they have completed their coaching programme, or several months later when they will have a more concrete idea of what has changed in their lives during the period after coaching. You might want to tell clients you approach for feedback that it is normal practice for you to do so. This will take the pressure off them and enable them to see your request as something natural and usual.

Having decided to approach your clients, you'll need to decide what questions you want to put to them. Consider the following two sets of questions which you could pose to a client on the completion of their coaching programme:

- How effective was the coaching programme at helping you reach your coaching goals?
- In what ways was it most effective at assisting you to reach your goals?
- In what ways was it least effective at assisting you to reach your goals?
- In what areas would you have liked further input?
- In what areas would you have liked different input?
- What areas of the coaching programme offered you least value?
- What other feedback do you have for your coach about the effectiveness of the programme?

- How would you describe the three most important strengths that your coach regularly displayed? Strengths are defined as positive factors which you observed or experienced in the way your coach ran the programme, built a coaching relationship with you and responded to your coaching needs.
- How would you describe the three most important areas for development that your coach regularly displayed? Areas for development are defined as negative factors which you observed or experienced in the way your coach ran the programme, built a coaching relationship with you and responded to your coaching needs.
- What would you have liked your coach to do differently and better during the programme?
- What other feedback do you have for your coach on their performance?

GETTING FEEDBACK ON YOUR PERFORMANCE

The first set of questions focuses on the effectiveness of the programme at reaching its goals. The second set of questions focuses on your competencies and performance as a coach. Either set of information could be vitally important for you, especially if a coaching programme hasn't gone that well and you want to learn from the experience.

There are plenty of other questions you could ask as well such as more detailed questions on:

□ specific aspects of your performance;

□ the extent to which your client thinks their coaching programme represents good value for money;

□ whether or not they'd be willing to provide you with a reference in future;

□ whether or not they'd want further coaching at some point.

All these questions are best posed via email or letter to give clients the option to think through their answers, and avoid the possibility of them feeling put 'on the spot' should you ask them face to face or over the phone.

It can be particularly useful for you to answer these questions yourself as well as asking clients. This way you can compare your clients' views of the effectiveness of their coaching programmes (or your performance as a coach) with your own view. The differences and similarities between these two sets of data can provide rich information for your own development programme, potentially highlighting areas in which you under- or overestimate your performance in comparison with your clients' views. You might like to start now.

Select a recent coaching programme you have run (or use a coaching experience from your coaching qualification course) and answer the following questions about your performance as a coach. You can use the space below each one to jot down your answer, or you may prefer to use a separate notebook.

❛ How would you describe the three most important strengths that you regularly displayed during the coaching programme (or coaching qualification course)? Strengths are defined as positive factors in the way in which you ran the programme, built a coaching relationship with your client and responded to your client's needs. ❜

❛ How would you describe the three most important areas for development that you regularly displayed during the coaching programme (or coaching qualification course)? Areas for development are defined as negative factors in the way in which you ran the programme, built a coaching relationship with your client and responded to your client's needs. ❜

What would you have liked to be able to do differently and better during the programme?

What else would you like to learn to improve your performance as a coach?

If you were answering these questions about a recent coaching programme you have run, from what you know of your client, to what extent might they agree or disagree with your assessment of yourself? Or, if you were writing about your performance on your recent coaching qualification course, you might like to ask some of your fellow course participants, or your course tutors, for their answers to these questions. If you wish you can jot down your answers in the space below, or you may prefer to use a separate notebook.

If you find that there are significant differences between how you assess your performance as a coach and how you think your clients or course tutors/participants assess it, you might like to consider what, if anything, you need to do to address the disparity.

WHICH CLIENTS TO APPROACH FOR FEEDBACK

Let's now turn to the issue of which clients to approach for feedback. In my experience this is not always as straightforward as it might seem. Some clients may be prepared to give you balanced feedback, which can be very useful indeed. Others may prefer not to provide feedback, or, depending on their skill sets, may not know how to. If they haven't had any other coaching experiences, they may not have a benchmark against which to evaluate your performance, and may simply not be able to provide effective feedback apart from the extent to which they did or did not find the programme helpful in assisting them to reach their coaching goals. Even if they have had other coaching experiences against which they are able to compare your performance, they may not feel inclined to make such a direct comparison. Some simply won't want to provide feedback, preferring to apply what they have learned and move on.

So, who can you approach? Basically, any client you think will provide you with effective, honest, balanced feedback from which you can learn – always respecting the fact that they might not want to participate in a feedback process.

Evaluating your own performance

Whether or not you decide to ask evaluative questions of your clients, you need to find supplementary ways of determining what you need to learn to do differently and better. Working with a supervisor is essential to this process, as is simply committing to a budget for your own continuous professional development. This section will focus on helping you decide for yourself in what areas you need to develop further as a coach.

Earlier on I asked you to evaluate your performance as a coach on a recent coaching programme or qualification course. Now I'd like you to step back further from your work and consider your wider development. In answering the following set of questions you might want to think about recent feedback you've had from your supervisor, or the last two or three coaching meetings you've run, or if neither or those options is feasible, consider what you learned, or are learning, on your coaching accreditation course.

The questions are designed to help you identify what you'd like to do differently and better in the future as a coach. You might like to use the spaces below each question to jot down your answers to them, or use a separate notebook.

What do you consider to be your overall strengths as a coach?

In what areas would you like to develop further skills?

What has been the most challenging coaching situation you've encountered recently? What was challenging about the situation? What would have helped you handle the situation more effectively?

What other coaching situation that you've encountered recently have you found challenging? What was challenging about the situation? What further competencies or skills would have helped you handle the situation more effectively?

In what areas in addition to those you are currently qualified in would you like to work as a coach?

> ❛ *Therefore, what training and skills do you need to acquire?* ❜

As you grow and develop as a coach so your coaching skills and competencies will grow and develop with you. Areas you currently find challenging and difficult may well become additional areas of strength for you as you work at improving in these areas. The areas for development you've listed above may well not apply to you in three or six months' time. So, it may be worth making a note in your diary now to revisit this development list in a few months' time to see what changes you need to make to it – and to keep track of your development in the meantime. You might also want to set yourself a deadline for developing yourself in these areas.

Membership of professional bodies

An obvious way to learn and develop is through joining one of the professional coaching bodies, meeting with other coaches, finding out what they are doing and making choices about what development opportunities you want to pursue. Membership of the main professional coaching bodies usually involves subscribing to a code of ethics, one of which relates to your standard of ongoing professional development. (See Useful Weblinks at the back of the book for a list of professional coaching bodies and their contact details.)

Increasingly, more and more development opportunities are available for coaches through the main coaching professional bodies, and many workshops, seminars and courses will be available to you as a member. It is well worth browsing their websites to see what they have on offer, how active their network is in your geographical area and what development opportunities they can offer you near your office base. Even if you are fully committed to a process of ongoing professional development, on occasions day-to-day work issues will inevitably compete for your time. Joining a professional coaching body, and participating in development activities through them, can be the prompt you need when you are busy and might be tempted to reprioritize your own development as less, rather than more, important.

Your ongoing professional development budget

It is important that you define and set aside a clear budget for your own ongoing professional development at the start of your budgeting period. As well as ring-fencing the funds for your development activity, you could also plan ahead by investigating the different development options available to you and booking places in advance at suitable events. Some coaches don't do this because they think that if they become busy, and they have already booked a place on a development activity, they will either not want to go, preferring to attend to their client work, or they will go but some of their attention will be on their client work. These coaches prefer to wait until they have a quieter patch before looking around for suitable development activities, hoping that something useful will be available.

I would encourage you to make plans for your more important development activities in advance by booking yourself on workshops, courses and supervision meetings well before the actual date of the activity. These dates will then be in your diary and you will not be available to book client work on them. As well as keeping the specific dates free when booking client work around these times, you will also need to keep free the dates either side of the development activity to give yourself some flexibility. Sticking to your planned development schedule will keep your skills up to date and you refreshed. Working this way will encourage you to:

☐ take seriously your commitment to develop yourself;

☐ see development activity as a priority;

☐ avoid the temptation, when push comes to shove, to use money that could have gone towards your development in another way.

SUMMARY

In this chapter we have discussed the importance of budgeting and planning for your own ongoing professional development so that you have new and fresh input to give to your clients. We've identified a few ways in which you might evaluate your current level of performance and so determine what development opportunities to pursue. And we've taken a brief look at how membership of one of the professional coaching bodies could contribute to your ongoing professional development cycle. Let's now examine your relationships with other coaches.

8

YOUR RELATIONSHIPS WITH OTHER COACHES

Part of what it means to be in employment is that you have colleagues to work with and get to know inside and outside of work. Since your colleagues were people with whom you worked day to day, and you all worked for the same employer, they were people with whom you had a vested, mutual interest in keeping your working relationships viable, at least under usual workplace circumstances. As colleagues, you worked in closely structured roles and towards the same overall workplace objectives. You contributed to the same stated cause: the success of your employing organization. In the normal course of your work together, you and your colleagues spent time and expended effort in working towards achieving similar, or at least related, goals. Consequently, among your colleagues, it is likely there would have been a pool of ready-made potential allies and co-workers – as well as some opponents and maybe even the odd enemy – with whom you would have developed effective working relationships, some friendships and plenty of social contact. For many of you, being part of a colleague network would have been an enjoyable and valuable part of your life.

Working as a sole practitioner isn't like that. Firstly – and most obviously – you don't have colleagues working in the same location as you, especially if you've decided to work from home. Secondly, you may not have any colleagues at all, depending on whether or not you are truly going it alone, and whether or not you are working as an associate coach. You may have a number of effective business contacts to draw on and you may have kept in touch with people from your coaching qualification course. But, if you do have enjoyable and effective peer contact with other people, the fact is that, even if you get on well socially, other coaches are often your competitors and often, as far as they are concerned, you are their competitor.

If you are someone used to plenty of social and workplace contact with other people and now find yourself searching for appropriate peers to talk to, this chapter is for you. It is also for you if you are likely to come into contact with other coaches while networking, while updating your coaching skills or in the normal course of your work. The chapter will help you to step back from your relationships with other coaches and decide where to put the boundaries so that you can enjoy fruitful, mutually beneficial contact with like-minded people on an ongoing basis.

Competition and boundary issues

It isn't always the case that every coach you meet is a competitor but in many cases it is true or certainly has an element of truth about it. It's all in the perception: both yours and theirs, and your two perceptions may not be the same. A life coach may not see an executive coach as a competitor at all, and vice versa. A coach specializing in working with technologists may not see a team-focused coach as much of a competitor either – until, that is, the team-focused coach starts to work extensively in the technology industry.

Geographic location also plays a part. You might not consider a coach who lives on the other side of the country to be a competitor of yours even if he or she works with a similar client base and with similar issues. But they might become one as far as you are concerned if they view travelling to work with clients as a normal part of the job and is prepared to work with clients anywhere in the country. So, basically, until you know differently, it is wise to assume that there will be at least some competition issues between you and other coaches that you come across. My advice is to tread cautiously when you first establish contact with other coaches that you'd like to cultivate a relationship with, at least until you have developed ground rules between you that will keep the relationship viable in the long term. What you don't want to do is to get your fingers burnt early on and become wary of engaging with other coaches in the future. That scenario could lead to you becoming professionally isolated.

Initial meetings with coaches

That being the case, the safest course of action is to hold back a bit whenever you meet a new and interesting coach – and there are many, many stimulating people working as coaches – until you are certain of the circumstances surrounding the person you have met. In particular, if you are hankering after a 'colleague' to talk to about general coaching issues or are just missing being part of a team at work, it can be tempting to treat other coaches as people on the same side as you. Unfortunately, that isn't always the way it works, so it is wise to be a bit circumspect, at least initially. Since some of the coaches you meet will, at least to some extent, be your competitors, any information you inadvertently give or candidly disclose about who you are working with, who you've made initial sales contact with, how you got in contact with them in the first place, how you intend to proceed and so on could be useful information to them. If you are very unlucky this may lead to you losing business, or at least to worries that you might do so.

However, not every coach you meet will be automatically on the look-out for nuggets of useful information from you – far from it. It won't even cross the minds of many coaches to think in this way and they will be quite happy to speak with you as someone working in the same field as them. Other coaches will only start to put up the shutters when something happens in a conversation to alert them to the possibility that the coach they are speaking with has a hidden agenda. You will find your own way, and your own intuitive sense of who you are dealing with will play a part in helping you establish enjoyable and productive contact with some coaches while leaving others well alone.

However, for your relationship with another coach to be viable, you need to be mindful of the potential boundary issues between you.

BOUNDARY ISSUES BETWEEN COACHES

Consider the following two instances:

☐ *A mutual coaching contact introduces you to another coach at a coaching seminar and the two of you decide to carry on talking after the event is finished. You both realize that you work with similar client issues and, as you are both starting out in your separate businesses, the other coach suggests that you could swap information about your coaching programme outlines and marketing materials, and give one another feedback. On the face of it, this is an interesting suggestion. You have been introduced to one another by someone familiar with you both and, as such, developing the relationship by you both giving and receiving feedback on the quality and content of your coaching programme outlines and marketing materials is an option you could pursue. You'd both have a chance to learn from one another and, hopefully, receive some suggestions for improving your written materials as well. However, there is also the possibility, even if it is remote at this stage, that the other coach wants to learn from your input and either not reciprocate at all or give less than effective feedback to you. She may want to take a look at your coaching programme outlines and marketing materials to see what ideas she could incorporate into her own work. Either of these outcomes could ensue and, until you have got to know the other coach a bit better, you won't know whether or not they will conduct themselves openly and transparently.*

☐ *Two coaches meet at a coaching network event and discover that they are working in close geographical proximity but focusing on very different client issues. They agree to meet again nearer their home bases and talk about their different businesses and approaches to coaching. One of them suggests, after a relatively short period of contact between the two of them, that they might sell, market and work together. Again, on the face of it, this is another interesting idea, one that might well be worth exploring further provided that it genuinely meets both coaches' needs. It would mean offering a more comprehensive coaching service to clients, one that encompasses two specialisms instead of just one, and should provide opportunities to learn from one another's skill sets, experience and knowledge. However, it will also mean being open with one another about which clients each of you is currently working with, which clients you are currently selling and marketing to and what other sales activities you have planned. That's all fine provided that the other coach respects the boundaries of your client relationships and vice versa, and working together in this way could be stimulating and rewarding for you both. But what if the coach making the suggestion has hit a rough patch, has lost confidence in his ability to sell and market, and is looking for another coach to bail him out and find him business? If this coach comes out and admits his problems that's one thing. But, if he doesn't, and therefore his offer of mutual selling and marketing is, to some extent, disingenuous, that could be quite another thing altogether. Of course, maybe working with a like-minded and supportive person is just what this coach needs to help him find his feet again. But if he doesn't at least describe some of his issues to the other coach, upfront and early on, then the second coach will be entering into a business relationship that might not deliver the promised joint selling and joint marketing activities, but will only result in him carrying his new colleague. Once more, either of these two outcomes could ensue, and only by putting your toe in the water will you get to know the other coach well enough to know whether or not working with him in this way will prove to be a good idea.*

Avoiding boundary conflicts

The politics of peer coaching relationships is complex and on many occasions coaches will establish mutually supportive and satisfactory working relationships with one another. They learn from each other, enjoy contact with one another and are able to add something to each other's businesses through their conversations. However, the possibility for boundary conflicts also exists and it's worth stepping back from offers to co-market, co-sell or co-deliver until you really know who you are dealing with and are sure that they work with similar values and in similar ways to you.

Networking with coaches who have a sufficiently different specialism to yours will mean that some of the potential boundary conflicts are obviated. This could be a less tricky way forward initially than networking with coaches who work with similar clients or in the same niche as you, and could provide you with contacts to whom you can refer your clients should they also want to work with a coach outside of your area of competence. However, the really important issues are the integrity, openness and honesty of the coaches you network with, and the quality of the relationship you strike up with them and they strike up with you, not simply the niche or locality in which you both work.

Establishing supportive peer relationships

Part of being your own boss and working as a sole practitioner is that you have chosen independence and autonomy as a way of life. With the freedom and choice that independence and autonomy bring comes at times a degree of isolation. If you are feeling too isolated in your work and would like supportive peer contact, the obvious thing to do is to go out and get in touch with other coaches. But, unfortunately, it is also the case that, even if you have developed an effective network of coaches and other business contacts, there will not always be someone available for you to speak with at any given time. Sometimes there will be, and sometimes there won't, and you will need to learn to live with a degree of discomfort from time to time when there are not peers available for you to talk to when you most need them. This is part and parcel of life as a sole practitioner.

In seeking out people with whom to establish effective and supportive peer relationships, you need to ask yourself what it is you are looking for and what it is that you would really benefit from professionally. You also need to consider what you can offer in return, how often you'd like to meet and for what purposes. Knowing these things upfront can make it easier for you to start off on the right foot, making it clear where you'd like the boundaries to be and what you expect and don't expect from the relationship, and clarifying what you want to give in return. In this way you are more likely to be able to manage your peer relationships effectively from the off, establishing and maintaining the kind of contact you'd enjoy and value professionally and personally.

You might like to think through some of these issues now by considering the following. You can jot down your answers in the space below each question if you wish to do so, or use a separate notebook.

What do you most miss about not having colleagues to work with?

❝ *What do you miss most about not having colleagues to chat with at work?* ❞

❝ *What kinds of issues would you most like to speak with a supportive coaching peer about?* ❞

❝ *What qualities are you looking for in a supportive coaching peer?* ❞

What can you offer to a peer in return for his or her support?

What would be a deal-breaker for you in a supportive peer relationship?

In order to establish the relationship along favourable lines, what else of importance to you do you wish to convey at the start of a peer relationship?

CONTACTING PROFESSIONAL COACHING BODIES

I would urge you to contact at least one of the professional coaching bodies and explore their ongoing professional development opportunities. The Useful Links section at the back of the book will point you in the right direction. You are likely to meet many interesting, stimulating and talented coaches in the course of your networking, ongoing professional development and other coaching-related activities. If managed effectively, these relationships should become a source of professional and personal enjoyment for you in your coaching business.

SUMMARY

This chapter has focused on the issues you need to consider as you establish and maintain effective peer relationships with other coaches. Let's now turn our attention to the ethical standards you need to take into account as a coach.

9

CLIENT CONFIDENTIALITY AND PROFESSIONAL ETHICAL STANDARDS

Your conduct as a coach is a matter for your own conscience and is something to which, as a professional advisor, you need to give some considerable thought. During the course of any coaching programme your clients may share with you information about the way they experience the world, what they want – and what they fear – from life or work, what they believe in and have anxieties about, how they see themselves and other people, as well as other private – and sometimes – confidential material. To make this level of self-disclosure viable for clients you need to ensure that you:

☐ make and keep strict confidentiality agreements with all your clients;

☐ adhere to the highest ethical standards in all your dealings with all your clients;

☐ set up and maintain appropriate boundaries at the start of each coaching programme – boundaries that make it possible for each client to make the best use of the time they have with you in any coaching meeting;

☐ keep any written materials that clients complete for you as part of their coaching programmes securely stored – these might include questionnaires and any other personal or revealing written records.

This chapter addresses the three interconnected issues of:

☐ respecting client confidentiality;

☐ working to strict ethical standards;

☐ adhering to current data protection legislation.

By the end of this chapter you will have examined how to handle these issues and understood how to stay the right side of the current data protection law.

Confidentiality issues

It goes without saying that, at all times, you must maintain the level of confidentiality that you have agreed with each of your clients. Different clients will want different degrees of confidentiality from you while for some clients confidentiality may not be an issue at all. However, respecting confidentiality agreements to the letter is essential for your reputation and your ongoing relationship with a client. Not many clients are going to want to work with a coach who leaves the coaching meeting and, on a subsequent occasion, tells other people what he or she learned about them, no matter how innocently or inadvertently the information is passed on. It could still be construed as a betrayal of trust and any client who knows that information they gave to their coach has been handled in this way would have the right to take the matter further if they wanted to.

DECIDING ON WHAT LEVEL OF CONFIDENTIALITY TO MAINTAIN

It is therefore vital that you, as a coach, make a clear distinction in your head between information that you have learned about a client that is definitely not to be repeated under any circumstances and that which you can safely talk about. Only you can decide where to put this mental marker. For example, you may decide that the safest place to put it is at 100%: nothing a client tells you, whether it is trivial, such as where they went on holiday last year, or grave, such as their concerns about their health or career, will be repeated by you outside the coaching meeting to anyone else under any circumstances whatsoever.

So, what level of confidentiality are most of your clients going to want to maintain? It all depends on the context of your work with them and their personal preferences. Let's look at the context of your work with them first. Most executive and organizationally based coaches set up strict and absolute confidentiality agreements with their clients. These written arrangements are agreed at the start of a coaching programme and state that everything that the coach and client say to one another inside a coaching meeting remains completely confidential but that the coach can, when asked to by a human resources sponsor or their client's manager, provide an update on the outcomes from coaching meetings, the action points that the client will take away from those meetings and the next steps for the coaching work. This way of working creates a balance between the needs of the:

- □ client who wants to speak openly and confidentially to their coach, knowing that what they say is said to the coach only and stays in the room;

- □ representatives of the client's employer who want to know what is happening in the coaching programme, what return they are getting on their investment, and what changes they can expect to see and by when as a result of the coaching work.

AGREEING CONFIDENTIALITY GUIDELINES

If you are working as a life coach, or in any other non-organizational coaching capacity, at the start of each coaching programme you still need to agree the confidentiality guidelines under which you will be working with your client. Once agreed these should be written down and given to each client so that he or she knows what to expect from you and has a copy of that agreement to refer to throughout the programme. In practice, most clients will not give issues of confidentiality a second thought once they have made a confidentiality agreement with you, unless and until something happens which causes them to have to do so.

Let's now look at the personal preferences of the client. Some clients do not worry about confidentiality at all and won't think to bring it up as an issue unless you do so first. For others, it could be a key deciding factor in whether or not they choose to work with you as opposed to another coach. You might therefore decide that you will always make confidentiality an issue for discussion during your initial sales meetings with potential clients. You could make a point of telling them that you'd like to work to boundaries and levels of confidentiality that suit them, before asking them how they'd like to structure these arrangements.

ABSOLUTE CONFIDENTIALITY

Let's work through an example and see what a client who demands absolute confidentiality might expect as a result of this agreement with you. Let's assume that you have been asked by a client to work with her and, as part of your contracting arrangements, you have agreed that everything you and she say to one another during her coaching programme will remain absolutely confidential. You have further agreed that all the information you learn about your client in the course of the research phase of the coaching programme – information given to you by her colleagues and contacts – will also remain absolutely confidential.

Remember that your commitment to absolute discretion in this case covers everything that is said to you:

☐ by your client;

☐ by anyone else that she puts you in touch with.

You can, of course, share any of the feedback you collect about your client from other people with *her*. But you cannot distribute information you learn about her to anyone else at all, in any context or for any purpose.

Why might a client want to work in this way? It is because she can only make best use of the dedicated one-to-one coaching time available to her with you, her coach, if she knows that what you say to one another will be treated with absolute discretion. It is an issue of trust on her part, and she is choosing to trust you, her coach, who she doesn't know and knew nothing about until you started to talk with her about her coaching programme. This client needs to make sure that her trust and self-disclosures will be respected by you. So she wants to place confidentiality parameters around the work that enable her to feel comfortable with the process and make it possible for her to commit wholeheartedly to it.

Confidentiality agreements

You may want to make it a standard part of your contracting procedure to distribute a confidentiality agreement to each of your clients, whether you work in an organizational context or with members of the public. If you do work as an organizational coach, you may also want to copy this agreement to anyone else who is involved with the coaching programme, such as your client's manager, the budget holder and any human resources sponsors. Alternatively, you may want to build a confidentiality agreement into your written coaching programme outlines which you are likely to distribute to every interested party anyway.

Any confidentiality agreement you decide to produce needs to be agreed first with your client. However, there are two instances when you may have to modify your confidentiality agreement. The first is where your client tells you something that leads you to believe that something illegal may be about to happen or may happen in the future. The second is if your client tells you about someone being hurt or in danger, or if you believe that they might be a danger to themselves. In either case you may be required to act on this information. It would therefore be wise to tell your clients when you make your confidentiality agreements with them, that if you become concerned about their safety, or someone else's, you will have to act despite the agreement. However, in 15 years of working as an executive coach I have not had to handle either of these sets of circumstances.

In formulating your confidentiality agreement you will need to include certain key points. Your confidentiality agreement could, for instance, state that:

☐ You have agreed the following way of working with your client, so that he or she can make best use of the coaching time available to them.

☐ In order to keep the boundaries of the coaching relationship clear, and to provide them with the confidentiality they will need to make full use of the coaching programme, you will keep each conversation between you absolutely confidential, except in the unlikely event that you become concerned about someone's safety or think something illegal may happen in future.

☐ This will also be true of any other information you learn about them during the course of your work, be it from questionnaires completed for you or contacts of theirs that you speak with or collect feedback from.

☐ If, during the course of the coaching programme, you speak with any of the coaching programme sponsors to provide them with an update about progress, you will not disclose any information your client has given to you, unless he or she agrees that it is OK to do so. You will instead focus the update on:
  – progress to date;
  – outcomes to date;
  – additional work to be done, if any.

If you are working with a member of the public you could omit the fourth bullet entirely, and write the confidentiality agreement in the first person before agreeing it with your client.

As an alternative to writing your own confidentiality agreement you might like to know that some of the professional coaching bodies require that their members adhere to the bodies' own codes of ethics. They also require that their members distribute a copy of this document to each of their clients at the start of each coaching programme as a written reminder of the standard of conduct that these clients can expect of their coach throughout the work they do together (see the Useful Weblinks section at the end of the book for more information).

In making your choices about how you want to handle confidentiality issues with your clients you might like to consider the following questions. If you wish, you can jot down your answers in the space below each question, or use a separate notebook.

> *Assuming that you are going to give each client a written confidentiality agreement, what do you want the initial draft of this agreement to say?*

At what stage of the sales or marketing process do you want to go through your confidentiality agreement with your client?

To whom, in addition to your client, will you copy the confidentiality agreement?

In addition to the coaching programme outline, where else in your sales and marketing materials are you going to introduce the confidentiality agreement?

Professional ethical standards

Confidentiality is just one of the professional ethical standards you will need to consider as a coach. There are others that you might like to commit to as well, as the following four ethical standards illustrate.

COMPETENCY

This means that you will only work with clients on issues that you are qualified to work with them on. It means that you need to be very clear in your own mind just where the limits of your competence lie, and be prepared firmly but kindly to tell a client who wants you to stray beyond them, that you can't. You may then want to go on to help that client find another coach or a practitioner who is qualified to work with them on those issues, or at least point them in the right direction towards finding suitable help.

PROFESSIONALISM

This means that you will not exploit your clients in anyway whatsoever and will work with them only on the issues they have agreed to work with you on. It also means that you recognize that your responsibilities towards some clients may extend beyond the termination of an initial coaching programme. This is especially true if you are helping someone with an ongoing process of change. In this case, as in others, you cannot simply walk away from a client if, at the end of your contracted work together, there is more work to be done without which your client will be unable to function effectively.

INTEGRITY

This means that you will act with honesty and transparency in all your dealings with your clients, upholding the law of the land and not saying or doing anything discriminatory.

BOUNDARY MANAGEMENT

This means that, since you will inevitably receive self-disclosures from clients during the course of your work with them, you must treat these communications professionally at all times. Also, should you suspect there may be emotional or commercial conflicts of interest between you and your client, or between you and your client's employing organization, you will address these quickly and effectively to make sure that your client's best interests are served. The coaching relationship between you and your client exists so that your client is free to speak about their coaching issues with you. It doesn't work the other way round, and it is simply not on – and may be very unhelpful – for you to open up to your client because you like them or feel rapport with them, and start talking with them about issues from your own life. The way you have, or have not, handled things are specific to you, and your client will not be helped by hearing about your personal story. Sharing information like this risks changing your relationship with that client from one thing into another, and may make it difficult for your client to go forward.

PUTTING IT ALL INTO PRACTICE

Wanting to work to the ethical standards you set for yourself is the first step. Behaving in ways that put these standards consistently into practice is what counts. Your supervisor will be well placed to help you see the wood from the trees should you ever need to talk through an ethical issue.

In deciding which professional ethical standards you want to work to you might like to consider the following questions. You can jot down your answer to each question in the space below it if you wish, or use a separate notebook.

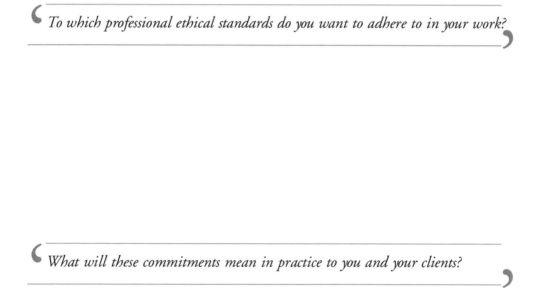

To which professional ethical standards do you want to adhere to in your work?

What will these commitments mean in practice to you and your clients?

❝ *How are you going to tell your clients about your commitment to these ethical standards of behaviour?* ❞

Data protection issues

The Data Protection Act 1998 applies to all personal information and is based on a set of eight principles. As they apply to a coaching business, these principles are not onerous but they are important and you do need to adhere to them. The law requires that you keep accurate and up-to-date data records for all your clients, that you handle and process all client data fairly and lawfully, and that you store all personal data, records and information pertaining to your clients securely. For any additional detail you might want on data protection issues see the Useful Weblinks section at the end of the book.

In deciding how you want to handle data protection issues – and other ethical issues that may concern you – you might like to consider the following questions. You can jot down your answer to each question in the space below it if you wish:

❝ *What provisions will you make to abide by the data protection legislation?*

"*Also, what other ethical issues concern you in addition to those discussed in the chapter?*"

"*How are you going to handle these issues in the future?*"

SUMMARY

We have taken a look at some of the ethical and confidentiality issues that you will need to consider as you set up and run your coaching business. Let's now turn to another key issue for your practice: how you set up and manage your business's finances.

10
MANAGING YOUR BUSINESS'S FINANCES

The reality of being your own boss is that you are now responsible for managing all aspects of your business's finances. This means that you must ensure that you:

- [ ] keep accurate records for tax purposes;

- [ ] file accurate tax returns each year;

- [ ] pay National Insurance contributions where appropriate;

- [ ] keep up-to-date and accurate VAT records, including completing and paying your VAT return every quarter if you decide to register your business for VAT;

- [ ] send out accurate and timely invoices to your clients;

- [ ] recharge the correct expenses from each of your clients as part of your invoicing procedure;

- [ ] keep all the business expense receipts you need for tax and VAT purposes, storing them for the time required by law and in an orderly fashion.

The ins and outs of the tax and VAT systems can seem complex and daunting at first, especially if you are not numerically inclined or not that interested in the details of the various financial accounting systems. However, even if your main focus lies in working with clients and you would like to get on with that aspect of your coaching practice, you will still need to engage with the tax and VAT systems, at least initially, in order to decide how to run your business's finances. Whether or not you work with an accountant in the long term, you will need to make a number of key financial decisions when you start off your business. These decisions will include whether or not you will:

- [ ] register your business for VAT;

- [ ] operate as a sole tradership or as a limited company;

- [ ] manage your business finances yourself, engage the services of an accountant or do both, assigning different roles to yourself and your accountant;

- [ ] purchase Income Protection Insurance and Professional Indemnity Insurance;

☐ purchase Public Liability Insurance as well as Employers' Liability Insurance, if you decide to run your business as a limited company;

☐ engage the services of an independent financial advisor to help you purchase the above financial products.

In addition, you will also need to consider how:

☐ often you will send out your invoices;

☐ you will handle unpaid invoices, assuming you are unlucky enough to have to do so.

Making sense of the complexity

This chapter is for you if, as a first-time business owner, the practicalities of managing your business's finances are something of a fog at the moment and you'd like a simple, straightforward guide to what you need to do and when. It's also for you if you'd like to understand which key financial decisions you need to make early on as you start to run your business. The chapter will take you through all the issues outlined above and examine the bigger picture in relation to each of them. You may like to consult one of the many excellent and informative websites on the finances of start-up businesses or speak with an accountant to gain supplementary information and additional detail on the tax, National Insurance contributions and VAT systems.

By the end of the chapter you should have decided how to manage your business's finances, so that you can focus with confidence on looking for and working with clients, knowing that you have already made the decisions and set up the processes that your business will need in the long run.

Sole tradership or limited company?

As a sole-practitioner coach you can run your business as either a sole tradership or as a limited company. Many coaches work as sole traders. Many work as the director of a limited company. The choice is yours, although the tax system treats each legal entity differently. The key points to consider when making your choice are as follows.

RUNNING YOUR BUSINESS AS A SOLE TRADERSHIP

Running your business as a sole tradership means that you are the only owner of the business and that you have complete control over the way in which the business is run. However, the law makes no distinction between the business's assets and your personal assets. This unlimited liability means that, should you incur a business debt, this could be met from your own personal assets – your home, your possessions and your savings, for instance. The benefits of setting up as a sole tradership are that registration is straightforward, your bookkeeping work can be kept to a minimum and you can keep all the profits after tax. You will need to pay Class 2 and Class 4 National Insurance contributions and file one personal tax return each year, but remember that the business's income (that is, your income) will be subject to the usual incremental tax bands which could mean you paying top-rate tax on some of your earnings if you have a good year.

RUNNING YOUR BUSINESS AS A LIMITED COMPANY

A limited company has employees, in this case probably one: you. The law makes a clear distinction between the assets of the entity called the limited company and the assets of its directors. This limits your liability as the director of the company and means that, unless you can be shown to have acted irresponsibly, should your business incur a debt, your personal assets will not be in jeopardy.

As the director of a limited company you will need to register your business at Companies House, appoint the company's officer(s) and shareholder(s), pay yourself a PAYE salary and/or dividends and keep general company accounts. The company will need to pay corporation tax on its profits each year, and both you and the company will need to pay Class 1 National Insurance contributions on your PAYE salary if it exceeds the lower earnings limit which currently in 2008-9, is £6,035. If the company also provides you, its director, with benefits in kind – such as a company car – the company will also need to pay Class 1A National Insurance contributions on the value of the benefits in kind. You will need to file a personal tax return each year, and the company will also need to file a corporation tax return each year.

The benefit of running your business as a limited company is that corporation tax is currently at a flat rate of 21% for 2008–9, provided that your company profits do not exceed £300,000 per year. This rate of corporation tax is called the Small Companies' Rate or SCR.

Keeping accurate records

This is essential: you must apply yourself to the discipline of keeping accurate records. The trick is having processes in place – be they paper-based or technology-based or a bit of both – that you use diligently and regularly to ensure that you are up to date with your record-keeping and bookkeeping. You will need processes for:

☐ retaining your business receipts for tax and/or VAT purposes;

☐ ascribing the right expenses to the right client invoice at the right time;

☐ sending out invoices in a timely fashion – and chasing late payments should you need to;

☐ recording what out-of-pocket expenses to reclaim for yourself from the company, if you are running your business as a limited company, so that you can offset them against profits; or recording what out-of-pocket expenses to offset against profits for tax purposes if you are running your business as a sole tradership.

Let's look at these issues one at a time.

RETAINING YOUR BUSINESS RECEIPTS

Every time you buy a product, incur travel expenses or pay a bill on behalf of your business you will need to keep the receipt as proof of purchase so you can offset the expense against profits and/or reclaim them from the business. All you need do is have a large envelope in your office drawer into which you diligently place these receipts at the end of each day. It's that simple. If you are registered for VAT, you will also use these receipts, on a quarterly basis, to complete your VAT return. So, you could start a new envelope each quarter. If you are not registered for VAT, you can replace your envelope whenever it gets full or on a regular basis such as monthly. Make sure you label each envelope with the correct period of time for the receipts inside.

ASCRIBING THE RIGHT EXPENSE TO THE RIGHT INVOICE

Secondly, you need to make sure that you ascribe the right expenses to the appropriate client invoice at the right time. You can do this simply and straightforwardly by having a folder on your computer for invoices, with individual client invoices in it, perhaps arranged year by year and month by month. Every time you incur an expense that you have agreed to recharge from a client, go into the appropriate invoice onscreen and make a note of the item and amount. Then put the receipt into your receipt envelope.

SENDING OUT TIMELY INVOICES

Thirdly, decide how often you want to invoice. Some coaches do so at each month end and invoice in arrears for the work done during that month. Others invoice on completion of each coaching meeting, either while they are with the client or afterwards via email or post. Others again invoice half-way through a coaching programme and again at the end of the programme. It depends on how often you want to invoice and on what invoicing schedule you have agreed with your clients. Keep hard copies of all your invoices and check these every now and then to see who has paid and who has not. You will also need to keep a record, on the hard copy itself will do, of when you received the money for each invoice into your bank account, or, if you are paid by cheque which you subsequently take to your bank, the date the monies are actually credited to your bank account.

RECLAIMING YOUR EXPENSES FROM YOUR BUSINESS

Fourthly, if you are running your business as a limited company, you'll also need to reclaim from the company any expenses you personally pay for while on company business. These expenses include those you probably won't go on to reclaim from a client (such as travel expenses for sales meetings) as well as those you will reclaim from clients (such as the cost of a questionnaire or booklets, for instance). You can do this simply by having a document on your computer called director's expenses on which you record each item, the date the expense was incurred and the amount involved. Having made this note, you can then go on to record the relevant expenses on your invoice for that client and put the receipt in your envelope as described above.

KEEPING ACCURATE RECORDS

Record-keeping isn't difficult. It's easy to understand in principle and straightforward to do in practice. What it does require is discipline to keep everything accurate in the long term. Handling your records effectively will:

- save you money when your accountant, if you hire one, works on your books, as they will have all the information they need when they need it and in the format they need it in;

- mean that you avoid the embarrassment of having to go back to clients to invoice for items you've missed off previous invoices;

- make sure that you reclaim from HM Revenue and Customs all the VAT and tax-allowable expenses owing to you, and that you reclaim from your clients all the items they have agreed to pay for.

VAT registration

The current threshold for VAT registration in the UK for the year 2008–9 is £67,000. This means that if your business turnover in any rolling 12-month period reaches £67,000, you are required to notify HM Revenue and Customs within 30 days of the end of month in which the yearly limit was exceeded. You must also contact them if your turnover in the next 30 days is expected to exceed £67,000. In either of these circumstances you are legally required to do the following:

☐ register for VAT;

☐ charge VAT, at the current rate of 17.5%, on all your subsequent invoices from the date of registration.

If you are not expecting your business turnover to reach £67,000 for the financial year you can still register for VAT on a voluntary basis. VAT registration entitles you to reclaim VAT, at the end of each quarter, on all the business expenses you have incurred during that preceding quarter. It also means that you need to work out how much to reclaim and to complete an accurate VAT return detailing this calculation each quarter. Depending on whether or not you want to do the maths yourself, you may need to hire someone to do this for you and your costs will increase. If you go down this route, you need to be sure that the amount you can reclaim will be, on an overall basis, more than the cost of getting the VAT return completed each quarter.

However, the benefit to you of registering for VAT is that you can reclaim the VAT on everything your business purchases that isn't zero-rated: for instance, your stationery and office supplies, the technology products and services you use, your accountant's fees, the gas and electricity you use to heat and light your office space, your business telephone charges and so on. Depending on your business's consumption of these and other VAT-rated products and services, it could be well worth your while to register.

DO YOU REGISTER FOR VAT OR NOT?

So, should you register for VAT or not if you don't think your turnover will exceed the VAT registration threshold? Remembering that being registered for VAT requires you to add 17.5% to all your invoices, you could say that the answer to the question depends to some extent on who your clients will be. If your clients are mainly likely to be companies rather than individual people, you could register for VAT on the basis that these client companies are likely to be VAT registered too, and so will likely reclaim the 17.5% you will have to add on to your invoices. But, if your clients are mainly going to be members of the public, charging an additional 17.5% might make some of them think twice about working with you if a coach of comparable quality is also available to them who doesn't charge VAT on their invoices.

However, having decided that you are going to register your business for VAT, you then need to decide which of the following VAT accounting schemes to go for: cash, annual or flat rate. The HM Revenue and Customs website has useful pages outlining the ins and outs of the various VAT accounting methods (see Useful Weblinks section at the end of the book). These pages are designed to help you select the method which makes most sense for you and your business.

Working from home or renting office space

Many sole practitioner coaches work from home. They have a dedicated room for their office work and meet with clients either at their clients' offices or at a neutral venue such as a hotel meeting room. Working from home entitles the coach to reclaim the appropriate proportion of their household bills as legitimate business expenses. These include the actual gas, electricity and telephone charges that relate to the business and the actual sundry repair and decoration bills for the office space. It also means that neither time nor money is spent travelling to and from work. Other coaches rent office space which affords them the option of working with clients at their own office if they want to and means that they can offset the full cost of running and maintaining their office as a legitimate business expense.

In making your choice about whether to work from home or to rent an office you might like to consider the following questions. If you wish you can jot down your initial reactions in the space below each question, or use a separate notebook.

To what extent is it important to you to keep your place of work and your home life in different locations?

To what extent do you consider the added costs of renting office space to be worth the possibility of leaving work behind at the end of the day when you return home?

> *How important is it to you to work with your clients away from their offices?*

> *To what extent do you consider the added costs of renting office space to be worth the opportunity to work with clients at your premises?*

Opening a business bank account

Even if you are going to operate as a sole tradership you should consider opening a separate bank account for your business. Having both your personal banking and your business banking going through the same account could result in you getting muddled and confused. If you are going to operate your business as a limited company you will need a separate bank account for the company anyway.

There are many, many bank accounts on offer to businesses. It is worth shopping around to see what deals you can get on bank charges, especially for BACS and CHAPS payments (inter-bank bill payments) and on the cheques that you write. It is normal practice for banks to charge a set amount for each business cheque you write and for each bill you pay via BACS or CHAPS. However, at any one time, at least one bank will be offering their new business banking customers free banking, even if only for a set period of time.

Many business accounts also offer telephone and/or internet banking facilities. These services mean that you can have access to your account 24 hours a day, 365 days a year, and can make transactions whenever you want without having to leave your office. Basically, make sure that the business account you open has all the facilities you want it to have. Your options include:

- a cheque book facility;

- a business debit or credit card;

- a facility to make BACS and CHAPS payments from your account;

- weekly or monthly statements sent to your office;

- 24/7 telephone banking;

- 24/7 internet banking;

- the option to move money between your personal and business accounts to pay yourself your earnings.

What insurance do you need?

At a minimum you might like to consider having both Professional Indemnity Insurance and Income Protection Insurance. If you are going to work with clients at your premises, you should purchase Public Liability Insurance and, if you are going to run your business as a limited company, it is compulsory for you to have Employers' Liability Insurance.

PROFESSIONAL INDEMNITY INSURANCE

Professional Indemnity Insurance is now compulsory for most professional businesses and services. These include professions such as architects, engineers, brokers, solicitors, independent financial advisors, accountants, computer consultants and so on. Working as a coach means that you are going to be advising your clients professionally on issues in their lives. As such, having Professional Indemnity Insurance is a must and, indeed, some of the professional coaching bodies require proof of your Professional Indemnity Insurance before they will accept you as a member. Professional Indemnity Insurance protects you and your business's interests against claims for error, omissions and professional neglect. It doesn't have to be an expensive insurance policy to take out, but it is an essential one to have.

INCOME PROTECTION INSURANCE

Working as a sole practitioner means that, should you be unfortunate enough to become ill and unable to work, or should you be injured and unable to work, your source of income simply ceases. It is also true to say that, should you return to work after either of these circumstances, it can take a while to build up your practice again. While Income Protection Insurance is not normally payable if you are back at work and looking to build up your business again, it can be vital while you are off sick and unable to earn income.

PUBLIC LIABILITY INSURANCE AND EMPLOYERS' LIABILITY INSURANCE

Public Liability Insurance covers you for any claims made against you by members of the public or other businesses (i.e. your clients) for any injury they sustain while working at your premises. However, it would not cover you should you be injured while working at your own office. This type of claim would be covered by Employer's Liability Insurance, which you need to have if you are running your business as a limited company. While Public Liability Insurance is generally voluntary, Employers' Liability Insurance is compulsory. You can be fined if you do not hold a current Employers' Liability Insurance policy which complies with the law.

WORKING WITH AN INDEPENDENT FINANCIAL ADVISOR

Given that there are so many different insurance products on the market, it might well be worth your while to engage the services of an independent financial advisor to help you find the product that is right for you. Most independent financial advisors will not charge you for their work. They earn their income through commissions payable by the insurance companies whose products they recommend. While this could lead some independent financial advisors to favour one product over another, you are not obliged to go with their recommendations and, should you decide not to proceed with a product an independent financial advisor recommends to you, you should not incur a charge for having done so.

Invoicing

There is certain essential information that you must include on all your invoices. If your business is registered for VAT you must show your VAT registration number on each of the invoices you send out. If your business is registered as a limited company, you must include your company registration number, your registered office and the place of registration as a legal requirement on all of your invoices. Each invoice must also have a date on it and should show your payment details and your payment terms (the number of days you are giving clients to pay the invoice) and include a unique reference number for that invoice. This numbering system is compulsory for VAT-registered businesses. You need to detail your fees and your agreed expenses separately, and in as much detail as you think necessary, so that clients know what they are paying for and won't need to query items on the invoice.

Handling late invoice payments

You may never have to handle a late invoice payment. Your clients may pay you on time, every time. But chances are that, sooner or later, you will have a client who doesn't pay up on time and you need to chase them. Once an invoice goes unpaid beyond your stipulated payment period (usually, but not always, 30 days) you need to contact your client again, remind them to pay up, send a duplicate invoice to help them make the payment speedily and hopefully that will be that. Sometimes, though, it isn't and you will need to send them a further letter. This letter should state:

- ☐ that the invoice is now overdue;

- ☐ by how many days it is overdue;

- ☐ that you don't want to have to treat it as a bad debt but that if it remains unpaid after a further period (usually one week) you will regretfully have to do so;

- ☐ that if they are having trouble with the payment perhaps they could contact you to discuss the issue and find a way forward.

If this still doesn't do the trick, you may have to treat the unpaid sums as a bad debt and take action against your client, unpleasant though this prospect may be to you. You could take them to the Small Claims Court yourself, or there are many agencies who can act on your behalf in circumstances such as these. Membership of the Federation of Small Businesses gives you access to such a service, as well as to many other services, and you will find a link to their website at the back of this book (see Useful Weblinks section).

Developing a business plan

The first question is: do you need a business plan? The purpose of a business plan is to provide you with a map or reference point which describes how your business is going to succeed and what you need to do to ensure that it does. As a sole practitioner coach you are unlikely to need investment or funding from a backer and your financial risks should be quite low, unless, of course, you are planning to rent or build new offices for yourself or are making a significant financial outlay in another part of your business. You are much more likely to regard yourself as the product you are selling and are likely to want to invest heavily in selling and marketing your business yourself in order to grow your business and make it a success. Therefore a business plan, if you decide to produce one, is really going to be of use to you and you alone.

You may decide that you don't need to invest time and effort in producing a written business plan, because your plans are all in your head and you are comfortable working that way. Alternatively, you may decide that a business plan will be a useful reference point for you, something that will prompt you into action and remind you of the direction in which you are going to go. How will you know whether or not to produce one? Maybe you don't need to invest in producing a business plan if you are clear:

- [ ] what you are going to do to set up and run your business;

- [ ] by when you are going to do these things;

- [ ] that the drive to bring your plans to fruition needs to come mainly from within you, and that you are comfortable working steadily towards your targets, mainly alone;

- [ ] that you are disciplined enough to work diligently and faithfully towards your business goals without needing a written reminder about what you are going to do and in what order.

But, if you are unclear about any of the essential aspects of running your business, or think that writing a plan will clarify them for you and subsequently keep you on track, maybe you do need to invest time in producing a detailed, comprehensive business plan. If you decide to do so make sure that it identifies:

- [ ] the key strengths and weaknesses of your business;

- [ ] the key areas where you need to develop expertise;

- [ ] the financial risks, if any, involved in setting up your business.

If you do decide to produce a business plan, you will need to review it on a regular basis. Updating your business plan as your business grows is important if it is to remain relevant to your evolving business's needs and priorities.

Working with an accountant

As a sole practitioner coach you need to decide just how solo you want to be. One very useful ally to have is an effective accountant – someone who defines their role as being to:

- [ ] save you money;

- [ ] help you handle your finances in the most tax-effective way;

☐ be on hand to answer the questions you are bound to have about what is tax allowable, what is not, which VAT system to use and so on.

Working with an effective accountant can save you time and headaches if you are not looking forward to your quarterly VAT computation or your annual tax return(s). However, working with an accountant will also put your costs up even if they are excellent at their job and therefore save you time and money through the quality of their advice. As an alternative there are excellent online sources of information about what is and what is not tax or VAT allowable.

It is a very personal decision and one that depends, to some extent, on the quality of the working relationship you have with your accountant, and the extent to which you value them for the contribution they make to your business.

In making your choice about whether or not to work with an accountant, you might like to consider the following questions. If you wish you can use the space below each question to jot down your answer or alternatively you may prefer to use a separate notebook.

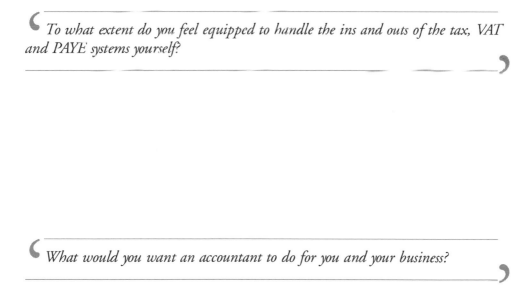

To what extent do you feel equipped to handle the ins and outs of the tax, VAT and PAYE systems yourself?

What would you want an accountant to do for you and your business?

' *What aspects of your business's finances do you not want an accountant to handle on your behalf?* '

' *To what extent do you think that the time you personally will save by employing an accountant will be better used by you in selling and marketing your business? Or working with clients? Or developing your skills and competencies as a coach?* '

EMPLOYING AN ACCOUNTANT

If you decide you do want to employ an accountant, you might want to draw up a set of criteria against which you will judge the effectiveness of the various candidates you interview so that you can be sure you are hiring the right accountant for you and your business. These criteria should include all the qualities and skills that matter to you in your choice of an accountant. At the end of the day, it's your decision and, as with every other aspect of starting and running your coaching business, whether you hire an accountant or not will depend on what you want to achieve and how you want to go about achieving it.

SUMMARY

We have taken a look at the key financial decisions you need to make in setting up and managing your coaching business. In the final section we will complete our examination of your coaching practice by focusing on the key points you need to keep in mind as you continue to sell to and work with your clients and potential clients.

FINAL THOUGHTS

Starting and Running Your Coaching Business

The work of a coach is rewarding, challenging and stimulating. Your role will create the opportunity for you to contribute positively to other people's lives. It will involve you in meeting new and interesting clients, potential clients and other coaches. It will require that you learn new skills and acquire additional knowledge on a regular basis. It will excite you, frustrate you and tire you out. It might also just be the most fulfilling workplace role you've ever had.

But, at the end of the day, the only person who is responsible for getting your business off the ground – and keeping it going along the lines you want – is you. To do this will require your tenacity, persistence, resilience and courage. You will need to:

- look at your business through the eyes of your clients on a regular basis and make sure that they see value in the way in which you do things;

- ensure that each and every coaching programme you run achieves its objectives in a timely and effective manner;

- work methodically at looking for new and better ways to market and sell your coaching services;

- manage yourself, your time and your energy so that you have more than enough to give to every client you work with.

Above all, however, the main focus of your energy and the majority of your time needs to be spent looking for clients to work with, and then working with them in ways they experience as effective and valuable. You will inevitably get sidetracked from time to time, and find that your energy and effort is taken away from these core areas of your business. But, after such an episode, you need to make a conscious effort to re-engage with the issues that you need to be most passionate about:

- telling your existing clients and potential clients how working with you on a coaching programme will benefit them, contribute positively to their lives and result in them achieving their coaching goals;

- delivering coaching programmes that add value to your clients' lives, achieve their objectives and do so in a way that results in your clients telling their contacts about how effective a coach you are.

Your experiences of running your business

I'd like very much to hear about your experiences of starting and running your coaching business. The following section, Useful Weblinks, will provide you with options for getting in touch with me and for contacting other organizations which might be able to provide useful input to your coaching practice. Whatever your background, coaching niche and personal circumstances, my hope is that this book has helped you organize your thoughts, harness your passion and set you on the path to running a coaching business that will change your clients' lives – and yours – for the better.

USEFUL WEBLINKS

On these pages you will find weblinks that you can use to help you get more detail on:

- what the various professional coaching bodies offer to and expect from their members;

- how to join a business network near you and what membership involves;

- the ins and outs of the tax, VAT and PAYE systems in the UK;

- organizations that work on behalf of small businesses, including how to learn more about the impact of current data protection legislation on your coaching business;

- how to get in touch with me to provide feedback on your experience of starting and running your coaching business.

Professional coaching bodies

To find out more about what membership of the different professional coaching bodies entails you might like to visit the following organizations' websites.

BRITISH PSYCHOLOGY SOCIETY SPECIAL GROUP IN COACHING PSYCHOLOGY

BPS is the representative body for psychologists in the UK and has a special group for psychologists – and non-psychologist affiliate members – involved in coaching. The BPS has responsibility for the development, promotion and application of pure and applied psychology for the public good, and its members are bound to adhere to the BPS Code of Conduct, Ethical Principles and Guidelines. Membership of the Special Group in Coaching Psychology is open to both psychologists and non-psychologists who are involved in coaching work.
http://www.bps.org.uk/
http://www.sgcp.org.uk/

ASSOCIATION FOR PROFESSIONAL EXECUTIVE COACHING AND SUPERVISION

APECS is a professional body for executive coaches and for the supervision of executive coaches. It is a not-for-profit organisation which provides accreditation for executive coaches and the supervisors of executive coaches; professional standards for executive coaching and the supervision of executive coaches; good practice guidance

and information about coaching and supervision; and information, events and resources for members.
http://www.apecs.org

ASSOCIATION FOR COACHING

The AC is an independent, not-for-profit organization whose goal is to promote best practice, raise awareness and raise standards across the coaching industry, while providing value added benefits to its members. The AC runs a series of co-coaching forums which meet regularly across the country. These meetings provide participants with opportunities to practise their coaching skills, network, promote good practice and receive peer supervision and feedback.
http://www.associationforcoaching.com/home/index.htm

EUROPEAN MENTORING AND COACHING COUNCIL UK

The EMCC exists to promote good practice and the expectation of good practice in mentoring and coaching across Europe. The public area of their website contains links to downloadable documents detailing their Code of Ethics, Diversity Policy, Complaints Procedure and Guidelines for Supervision. EMCC members must abide by their Code of Ethics, provide each client with a copy of this document at the start of each coaching programme and be in ongoing professional supervision while they work as a coach.
http://www.emccouncil.org/

INTERNATIONAL COACH FEDERATION

The ICF has members in over 80 countries. It works to develop the standards of the profession, establish a career structure for coaches, support its member coaches through conferences and other development forums, and help people wanting to work with a coach find someone suitable through its referral service.
http://www.coachfederation.org.uk

Business networks

To find out more about business networking opportunities in your area you might like to visit the websites of the following organizations:

THE BUSINESS NETWORK

The Business Network holds monthly lunches in major towns and cities throughout the UK. The lunches bring together decision makers to promote their businesses and expand their network of local and regional resources in a structured two-hour session.
http://www.business-network.co.uk

BUSINESS NETWORK INTERNATIONAL

The BNI is a business and professional organization that allows only one person from each trade or profession to join each chapter. Members all carry one another's business cards with them and look for opportunities to make referrals on behalf of fellow chapter members.
http://www.bni-europe.com/

HM Revenue and Customs

HM REVENUE AND CUSTOMS

HMRC is the government body that handles the tax, VAT and PAYE systems in the UK. Their website provides full information on all the ins and outs of the different systems and is surprisingly user-friendly.
http://www.hmrc.gov.uk

Small businesses organizations

FEDERATION OF SMALL BUSINESSES

The FSB represents the interests of small and medium-sized businesses in the UK. Members have access to a comprehensive set of business services including a range of insurance products, banking products, telephone services, medical services, credit card services and so on. Members also can also call on the services of a firm who will recover bad debts on their behalf.
http://www.fsb.org.uk/

BUSINESS LINK

Business Link provides practical support, data and advice for businesses. Its website has comprehensive, up-to-date information on many business-related issues such as tax returns and payroll, IT and e-commerce, growing your business, and sales and marketing. It also has information about the current data protection law and how to comply with it. Use the search facility on the homepage to find the relevant pages on what the Data Protection Act means to you and your business.
http://www.businesslink.gov.uk

Aryanne Oade

To tell me about your experiences of starting and running your coaching business, or to explore options to help you develop further as a coach, you might like to visit:
http://www.oadeassociates.com

INDEX